New Tools

FOR A

New Century

FIRST STEPS IN EQUIPPING YOUR CHURCH FOR THE DIGITAL REVOLUTION

John P. Jewell

ABINGDON / NASHVILLE

NEW TOOLS FOR A NEW CENTURY:
FIRST STEPS IN EQUIPPING YOUR CHURCH FOR THE DIGITAL REVOLUTION

Copyright © 2002 by Abingdon Press

This book is printed on acid-free paper.

Library of Congress Cataloging-in-Publication Data

Jewell, John P., 1938–
  New tools for a new century: first steps in equipping your church for
the digital revolution / John Jewell.
    p. cm.
1. Church work—Data processing. I. Title.
BV652.77 .J49   2002
254´.3—dc21   2001008573

Scripture quotations, unless otherwise indicated, are from the *New Revised Standard Version of the Bible,* copyright © 1989, by the Division of Christian Education of the National Council of the Churches of Christ in the United States of America. Used by permission. All rights reserved.

Scripture quotations marked (NIV) are taken from the HOLY BIBLE, NEW INTERNATIONAL VERSION ®. NIV ®. Copyright © 1973, 1978, 1984 by International Bible Society. Used by permission of Zondervan Publishing House. All rights reserved.

Microsoft® Windows®, Windows® 3.0, Windows® 95, Windows® 98, Windows® 2000, Windows® NT, Internet Explorer®, Outlook Express®, PowerPoint®, FrontPage®, FrontPage® Express, and Microsoft Office® are either registered trademarks or trademarks of Microsoft Corporation in the United States and/or other countries.

Screen shots reprinted by permission from Microsoft Corporation.

Netscape and the Netscape N and Ship's Wheel logos are registered trademarks of Netscape Communications Corporation in the U.S. and other countries.

02 03 04 05 06 07 08 09 10 11—10 9 8 7 6 5 4 3 2 1

MANUFACTURED IN THE UNITED STATES OF AMERICA

For Janell and Jennifer

Contents

Contents

PART FOUR: HOW TO GET THERE FROM HERE

Introduction

"Toto, I've a Feeling We're Not in Kansas Anymore"

There is a wonderful line in *The Wizard of Oz* where a wide-eyed and somewhat frightened Dorothy has just landed in the land of Oz. She is spellbound as she clutches her little dog Toto in her arms. You are gripped by a marvelous sense of innocent wonder in Dorothy's voice as she says, "Toto, I've a feeling we're not in Kansas anymore."

I think of Dorothy's experience when I talk with people about all that is possible using technologies that are available for use in our churches today. Technology is not new for me. Just over thirty years ago a brand-new IBM 360 was installed at our IBM-owned data processing company. The computer and peripheral equipment required a twenty-five-hundred-square-foot room with an elevated floor that concealed hundreds of yards of cable and electrical equipment.

Times have changed! The laptop computer that sits on my desk takes up about one square foot and is one hundred times more powerful than that IBM 360.

In terms of the technological world our children are entering, we are most certainly "not in Kansas anymore." Even though I have a strong technology background, I find myself in wonderment over the pace at which our younger folk learn and use technological tools. Have you ever attempted to defeat one of your children at the video arcade on *any* game?

In spite of all my familiarity with things technical, my then four-year-old daughter left me amazed one morning about a year ago. She had pestered me to let her play with "Sesame Street Elmo's Preschool" on my computer as I was getting ready to go to work. We had spent some time together during the previous week so she could learn the basics of using a mouse and getting around the program.

When we began exploring the computer, it was immediately apparent that children and adults have radically different approaches to technological learning. My daughter, Jennifer, *leaped* toward the keyboard when I invited her to try it out. My wife, on the other hand (who declared her interest in the computer to be similar to her interest in accompanying me to Sears to pick out new tires for the car), approached our computer as a bomb squad might approach a suspicious package. It was essentially the difference between "Let me at it!" and "This thing scares me to death!"

Back to the morning my little girl left me with mouth wide open. I allowed her to continue exploring her game while I went through my morning routine. She had been exploring a part of the program where one finds treasures by searching various parts of a castle. I was not able to help her complete the treasure hunt, because it became a bit tricky and I was in a hurry. When I returned to help her, I was stunned to see that she had found the pot of gold, the final treasure! "How did you do that?" I exclaimed.

"Well," she answered, "you have to click here . . . then go through this window . . . and wait for the treasure to come. . . . See, there it is!"

I was nonplussed. Dorothy was right: "Toto, I've a feeling we're not in Kansas anymore." This experience was one of those defining moments when reality takes on a new configuration. Our entry into the new world was cemented for me when my now six-year-old daughter and I were shopping at her favorite department store. One of the joys of her life used to be looking through the toy department.

"Would you like to look at the toys before we go home?" I offered.

"No," she answered, "but can we look at the software?"

If the phenomenon Alvin Toffler called "future shock" had an impact on my generation, Jennifer's generation must certainly be experiencing "present shock." The shifting ground of reality is not the pace of change, but the normalization of rapid change that has an impact on the lives of contemporary people. For Toffler's generation, the issue was the sometimes difficult struggle in adapting to the pace of change. Today's children experience change as the norm and inability to deal with change as abnormal. This leaves adults in Kansas and children in Oz. We are, without a doubt, living in the midst of a revolution akin to the industrial revolution. The only exception being the fact that *this* revolution will bring about more change in less time than the latter.

Think for a moment about our youngest generation. They will have absolutely no idea of what a world without CDs, CPUs, "dot-coms" or the Internet was like. The photographs of CEOs that will adorn the hallways of the corporate headquarters of their future will frequently be of men and women (in equal numbers) in their late twenties and early thirties. The word *windows* will make them think of software, and the thought of a "crash" will create a strong desire for "backup." Even now, when two or three of this generation are gathered together in conversation about their computers, many of us haven't a clue what they are talking about.

One of the signs that we have truly entered a new age is the anguished look that many parents have on their faces when they come to me as their pastor and say, "My kids want us to get on the Internet. What should I do?" The children long for access. Parents dread it. The clincher that we have entered a new age is that some children and teenagers consider the lack of Internet access at home practically the same as child abuse, or at least child neglect.

The past few years have made it clear that we in the church have no choice but to engage the question "What shall we do with the digital revolution?" The landscape for ministry has been forever changed. All absolutely wild predictions about the growth of the Internet and the impact of technology on our lives have fallen far short of what has actually taken place. Our children are growing up in a world where new technologies will have a profound impact on the social, intellectual, physical, and emotional dimensions of their lives.

Think about a few of the ways their world will likely be different:

- They will mature in a world where human organs for transplant will be grown in medical laboratories, and they will carry their complete medical histories in tiny computer chips beneath the skin. Should they need surgery, a surgeon in New York could perform the operation in Kansas through a computer-directed robot.
- Most of them will work for several institutions during their careers, many of them will work for themselves, and three years with any one company just might place them near the top of the seniority list.
- Education and learning will be lifelong. While retraining was a necessity in the last three decades of the twentieth century, work life will be characterized by continuous learning. Retraining will be seamlessly woven into the fabric of career.
- The economy will be driven by electronic commerce and most financial transactions will take place on the home computer. A trip to the bank could well be an annual event to check on the safe-deposit box.
- Lines between home, work, and leisure will continue to blur. It will require a strong discipline to keep the boundaries of home, work, and play separate.
- When our children become parents, they will carry devices similar to cell phones. But these units will be capable of voice and data communication that will start their cars, turn on the air conditioning in their homes, page their children, check their audio-video email, and maybe upload a few pages to their Internet sites. These will be personal command centers that can be carried in a shirt pocket.
- Christianity will become a minority religion in the United States as the total number of people who identify themselves as Christians will fall below 50 percent of the population.

The likelihood is that these notions fall short of what will actually take place. It can be very intimidating for people who are not all that familiar with new technologies. We may not be in Kansas anymore, but Kansas is not a bad place. Even Dorothy wanted to go back home. Oz was wonderful, but when all was said and done, she closed her eyes, clicked her heels together, and spoke her wish, "There's no place like home. There's no place like home." The only problem is, we can't go back. We can click our heels all we want and wish for the days when a window was something you looked through, a crash was something that happened to cars, and a mouse was that little creature you set a trap for. The world and particularly our children are "wired" and "connected," and we have no choice but to respond.

The question has to be asked: Is this a better world our children are entering?

Absolutely.

Young people today are living on the threshold of astonishing achievements in every aspect of their lives. The term *global village* is no longer a simple phrase; technologically, it is a reality. Words like *cancer,* which strikes fear into our hearts today, could be a bad memory in their adult years. They will be more educationally advanced in their beginning high school years than we were at college graduation.

But wait a minute. Is this also a worse world?

Absolutely. At least, there are new dangers in this world.

The CBS newsmagazine *48 Hours* broadcast an episode called "Cyberstalker," which detailed some of the horror stories and dangers of life online. Our children are at risk when they enter chat rooms or give out information in emails or on interactive Web sites. Advances in medical research and development bring more serious questions about human values and ethics. There is no longer a question about *whether* we will be able to clone human beings, but *if* we will actually engage in human cloning. Our grandchildren will witness the human life span nearing 120 years. The question is what they will *do* for 120 years. We can even ask *where* they will live. Will it be on planet Earth or some other place in space? Daniel S. Goldin, administrator of NASA, believes that we will land on Mars "in no less than 10 and in no more than 20 years."[1] The questions can reasonably be raised: If we are not able to manage a 70-year life span, what are we going to do with a 120-year life span? And, If we cannot live peaceably on this planet, what exactly is it we will be spreading to other planets?

The fact is that we have entered a new century and a new millennium that are neither better nor worse than the century and millennium we have left. The issue is not so much what kind of world we are entering, but what kind of persons are entering the world to be. There is potential for incredible good, and there is potential for incredible evil.

The technological revolution that is upon us is nothing more or less than a new mission field, and it is incumbent upon those of us who love the church and its Lord to "ask the Lord of the harvest to send out laborers into his harvest" (Luke 10:2). My personal belief—no, passion—is that it would be irresponsible of us to fail in equipping ourselves for this new challenge. Faithfulness to the Lord of the harvest requires that we prepare ourselves to bring some of the new technological tools' potential to our outreach, educational, and worship ministries. Even as we answer the call to this mission field, we are only doing what is expected of disciples. Consider the needs of our children and teenagers who are already out there in cyberspace and you can almost hear the voice of the Macedonian in Paul's vision: "Come over . . . and help us" (Acts 16:9).

* * *

I need to say just a few words about how this book is organized. The primary purpose of these pages is to help the "This thing scares me to death!" church in its ministry to a "Let me at it!" generation.

Part One: "Boot Camp." This section covers basics for those who are new to the world of computers and the Internet. This section can be skimmed by those who have some knowledge of the basics and skipped by people who would describe themselves as intermediate computer users. "Skip Quizzes" in this section are short quizzes you may take to let you know that you can skip the chapter. For those who may be introducing this material in the local church, the "Skip Quiz" could be used as a teaching tool.

Part Two: "Preliminaries." This includes a message to parents, pastors, and lay leaders in the church. I discuss some of the spiritual/theological issues surrounding technology and its use in the church, along with some reflections on how the culture has changed. There is some discussion of special concerns for pastors, parents, and lay leaders.

Part Three: "New Tools for Ministry." This is an introduction to the equipment needed to make use of new technologies and how this equipment relates to the familiar audiovisual equipment most of us are used to. Following this I offer some help in getting familiar with the software or programs used in preparing material. I conclude with some specific information about putting the material to use in youth ministry and education, worship, and Internet-based ministry.

Part Four: "How to Get There from Here." Part Four is a final reflection on the meaning of this new field of technology for the church and especially for the ways we think of ministry. There is a discussion of administration and planning for program implementation in the local church. I will discuss budget considerations along with planning a time frame for implementation. This section concludes with a chapter called "Ideas You Can Use in Your Local Church," which is an assortment of ideas that can easily be transferred to your local ministry.

The charts and quizzes in this book are available on a companion Web site located at *www.newtools-online.com*. You will be able to print these and other resources and reproduce them for use in your local church. The Web site also contains both links to the resources mentioned in this book and other resources. The links section is organized to parallel the chapters of the book.

Part One
BOOT CAMP

Your kids finally did enough begging to get you to buy a computer, or your colleagues told you your typewriter was last century's technology and you should be getting help from the Internet for your sermons anyway. You look at the Sunday newspaper ads for computers and haven't a clue what to buy. Now what?

Chapter One

Really, Really Basic Computer Stuff

Skip This Chapter?

If you are familiar with purchasing a computer and software, you may be able to skim or even skip this chapter altogether. Go to the Appendix and take Skip Quiz #1, then decide whether you can skip or skim this chapter or if you should study it as a basis for the rest of the book.

Components of a Basic Computer System

Finally, you've made the decision! Whether alone or with your co–decision maker or makers, you spread out the Sunday ads or head for your favorite electronics or office supply superstore.

"Gulp!" You can get a computer for anywhere from $799 to $2,999, and you haven't a clue why the one for three thousand dollars is different from the one for eight hundred dollars. You can actually spend thousands more than this for your computer, but most systems you will consider for adequate home use will run between $1,000 and $2,400.

Now comes the first inkling of a new language you will need to learn. At an absolute minimum, you have to sort out the differences in things like MHz, MB, RAM, CD-ROM, and modem. The confusing thing is that all the computer systems look essentially the same. You can't tell anything about RAM, MHz, MB, and all the rest just by looking at the computer.

I suggest four steps in going from your first look at the computer to picking a basic computer system for your purposes.

1. What do you see on the shelf or in the ad?
2. What are those mysterious terms like *megahertz* (MHz) and *RAM*?
3. Which computer should you buy?
4. What do you need besides a basic computer system? (The things we call peripherals.)

But first, there are two housekeeping items you need to take care of. One thing to realize is that there are two major types of computer systems commonly known as the personal computer (PC; IBM compatible) and the Macintosh. IBM originally designed the basic format of the PC. As other companies developed computers for personal use the terms *IBM compatible* and *IBM clone* were coined. The other major computer company then was Apple, which has become known for the Macintosh computer. Apple computers were widely used in schools, and the descendant Macintosh systems continue to be used. The mainstream will continue to be the PC for the foreseeable future. There are still people who love to debate the merits of the PC versus the Macintosh. For them, it is a kind of Hatfields and McCoys thing.

This text will focus on the PC. The PC is by far the most widely used system for home and business. There is significantly more software written for the PC and more readily available technical support for the PC than for the Macintosh. When asked about the choice between the two systems, I almost universally recommend the PC as preferable for most use.

The second issue has to do with laptop computers. I will not be discussing laptops in this chapter other than to say that the basic components are similar to "desktop" systems. My recommendation to most people is that their first computer system be a desktop system. "Desktop" system means simply a computer that will stay at home on your desk. (The exception to this is when you have no choice but to do your computing in several different locations, or you do a lot of traveling and need to take your computer with you, which might necessitate your purchase of a laptop computer.)

For most people the search for a suitable computer will result in purchasing a desktop PC.

Now, on to the selection process.

What Do You See on the Shelf or in the Ad?

When you look at the ads or on the shelf in the store, every computer will have four basic components. They come in different shapes and colors, but every one will have a box, a monitor (looks like a TV screen), a keyboard (resembles the old typewriter), and a mouse (the smallest part that looks a little bit like a mouse, especially with the wire that some folks thought resembled the mouse's tail).

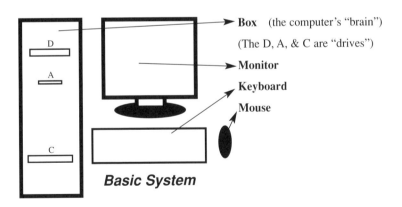

Figure 1a

Figure 1a shows the basic components that make up a computer. Without all of these items, you have computer parts but not a computer system. The box (or brain) does the processing (or thinking). The D, A, C on the box represent drives the computer needs in order to operate. I will talk more about the drives in a bit. The monitor is the system's vision (it lets you see your work or the game you are playing). The keyboard allows you to talk to the computer. These components constitute a computer system.

There is one additional bit of equipment called a mouse. The mouse also lets you talk to the computer. A few years ago, the mouse was an optional piece of equipment. You could do everything you wanted by using the right combination of keys on the keyboard, but the mouse made things easier. When you move the mouse, a small arrow on the screen moves to various places where you can click the mouse and make the computer do your bidding. People call this the point-and-click method of making the computer do things.

You can compare the way the mouse works to the remote control found on some automobile key chains. There was a time when you had to walk to your car, take the keys out of your pocket or purse, put the key in the lock, unlock the door, and then open the door. Now, with a remote control, you can point and click. The car unlocks automatically. Some of those remote controls are pretty fancy and you can open your trunk or even start the car from inside the house on a cold winter morning. All with a point and click. Likewise, the mouse has made moving around the computer so much easier that it has earned a place in the basic computer system configuration.

There is another component you will most likely want to add to your basic system. If you plan to write letters, papers, or print pictures, you will need to add a printer to the basic system. Many computer systems come with printers, and I will discuss printers in depth later in this chapter.

What Are Those Mysterious Terms Like *MHz* and *RAM*?

READING THE LABELS

The $799 computer system and the $2,999 one look very much alike. Why the price difference? To understand, you will need to read the label or description of each computer. There are five bits of information usually displayed in describing the computer that are important to understand when you buy. It will look something like this:

Figure 1b

In order to read the labels, you want to know these terms and what they mean:

MHz: This has to do with how fast the "brain" of the computer will process the information it is working with. This brain is called a central processing unit (CPU). If you are simply going to write letters and papers with your computer, you won't notice the difference between the 650 MHz and the 900 MHz processors. If, however, you plan on playing video games or working with lots of photographic files, you will notice the difference. The speed of processors has gone from 60 MHz to over 1800 MHz in just the last few years. The least expensive systems now come with at least 500 MHz, which is adequate for most home use. (These numbers change quickly. You should check the companion Web site for current information.)

Just one note of caution here. The label above that says $799 displays what many would consider minimum requirements for most users. Beware of the hand-me-down from Uncle Joe, who has just upgraded his computer and wants to give his older one to you. Your children will try to play one of their games on Uncle Joe's old computer and run into problems. They will give you a really hard time when the processor won't process fast enough and the computer's memory runs out of room. The next thing they'll see is a blue screen and a message that says something like, "NOT ENOUGH MEMORY!"

RAM: This stands for "random access memory." You could compare this to the size of a desktop where you have to write your letters, balance your checkbook, and do your taxes. If you are simply writing a letter, a small desk is just fine. But when you do those taxes every year, you want the biggest desktop you can find. Otherwise you are running all over the room carrying files, notes, and receipts back and forth to your desk. This is what the computer has to do. It needs to have the files and information available on the desktop so it can randomly access what it needs to do the work. When you do your taxes and have the luxury of a really big desk, you can access your receipts and other papers randomly. When the computer is working with photographic files, for instance, it wants a large desktop. If the desktop (RAM) is too small, you will have to sit and wait while the processor (CPU) runs back and forth to the file cabinet to get the information.

The computer's desktop, or amount of room it has to work with files without having to go to the "file cabinet," is measured in "megabytes" (usually stated as MB). A megabyte is tech talk for one million bits of information. A million bits, or one MB, seems like a lot, but for a computer it isn't very much. The standard for RAM has continued to grow as the years have passed. A year ago the minimum was 32 MB. (That is, 32 million bits of information can fit on the desktop.) Most systems now come with 64 MB, and by the time you read this 128 MB may be standard.

The reason RAM is so important is that when the information your computer wants to process is not available on the desktop (that is, available at random), it has to be stored in the computer's file cabinet, which is called the hard drive. RAM is relatively inexpensive and easy to install. Personally, if you can afford the expense now, I believe RAM is where you get the biggest bang for your buck. With the size of most programs today, you should probably aim for a minimum of 128 MB of RAM.

Hard Drive: The computer's file cabinet or hard drive is measured in GB, or gigabytes. Not so long ago, the hard drive was measured in MB, but as you are probably beginning to figure out, the file cabinet has to hold tons more information than it used to and now it is measured, not in millions of bytes, but in billions of bytes.

Most computers now come with 20 GB and this is good for most home use. If you have three or four teenagers who will be storing lots of video games and you want to store the family photo albums in the computer, then it would be a good idea to get more hard drive space.

The hard drive also contains all the programs (software) you will be using. More programs will require more space. The hard drive is more difficult to upgrade. You can't add more file cabinet space, so you would need to get a new cabinet (hard drive). It's best to get what you need at the beginning. I will discuss this a bit more later.

In Figure 1a, the box has little rectangles labeled "D," "A," and "C." The one labeled "C" represents the hard drive. It is inside the box and you don't physically access this drive. The program that tells your computer how to function and what to do is located here. When the computer starts up, your monitor will (in most cases) show you a screen called a window. These windows will set everything up so you can begin to work (or play) on the computer. Once this screen is displayed, you can literally move in and out of your work through little windows. Tech talk for turning your computer on and waiting for it to get your programs ready for work is to "boot" your computer. When you boot your computer, your hard drive ("C" in Figure 1a, actually called the "C drive" most of the time) goes to work and gets you ready.

The drive I've labeled "D" in Figure 1a is the CD-ROM drive. Understanding this term is easy enough really; it stands for "compact disc–read-only memory." This drive is one you physically use. The discs that fit in the drive look just like a music CD. In fact, in most computers you can play a music CD using this drive. This drive also will read CDs that have programs on them. The ROM part (read-only memory) means that your computer can read the information on the disc, but can't write anything on the disc or store anything on it. (There are CD drives that can write on CDs, and I will discuss this a bit later.) A computer uses CDs as a way to get information such as the programs you will use on the hard drive.

The drive that is labeled "A" in Figure 1a is called a floppy drive. This is a bit of a misnomer because the disc that goes into this drive is a little 3.5" by 3.75" thing that isn't really floppy. The term *floppy* originated a few years ago when computers used flexible discs that were about 5.5" square. The name *floppy* stuck, and now those 3.5" stiff things are called floppies and the drives they go into are called floppy drives.

Most computers assign the letter "A" to the floppy drive, which is also called the "A drive." Floppy discs are the best place to save your work if you want to bring the work to another computer. Floppies can also be used by computers to load information to the hard drive, but most programs now come on CDs. This is mainly because programs are larger and one CD will hold 448 times as much information as a floppy disc.

Modem: You will not need the modem in your computer until you choose to use email and surf the Internet. (Of course you bought the computer because you want email and access to the Internet, and almost all computers come with modems.) A modem is the piece of equipment that enables your computer to talk to another computer. Computers talk to one another through telephone lines. The numbers associated with modems have to do with speed. A 56K modem will allow 56 thousand bits of information to pass from another computer to yours. Actual speed is affected by a number of factors, so you won't actually connect to the Internet at 56K. It's kind of like an automobile that is rated to go one hundred miles per hour, although road conditions, traffic, and other factors come into play and most of us will never travel at one hundred miles per hour in our cars.

The speed of telephone connection to the Internet using a modem is stuck at 56K right now, and this is pretty much the standard. Don't buy anything with less than a 56K modem. It is possible to connect to the Internet through cable or special phone lines, and I will discuss this a bit more in the section dealing with the Internet.

How the Computer Thinks and How You Talk to It: Software

Here's a bit of information you will enjoy. Computers are not very smart. In fact, they are actually quite unintelligent. If you want to check this out for yourself, you can do so the moment you get your first new computer. Plug the thing in and tell it to write a letter or add up a column of numbers. It will just sit there!

Your computer cannot do anything without very thorough instructions. These instructions, or "programs," do two basic things:

1. The program that tells the computer how to function and coordinates all the parts of the system (monitor, mouse, printer, drives) is called an operating system. (It operates your computer.)
2. Programs that do work for you, like word processing or accounting, are called applications or applications software. Games and learning programs your children will want (especially the games) are also applications software.

The key thing to remember is that the computer cannot write the letter or do your accounting without instructions and without your input. If you tell the computer to deduct five dollars from your checkbook when the actual number should have been seven dollars, guess what? The computer hasn't a clue!

Do you see? The computer doesn't know anything except what you tell it or what a program tells it. When a program isn't working properly or wrong information is given to the computer, it will just blindly go along with the program.

Why would anyone want a machine that doesn't have an original thought? The answer is speed. The computer can't think for itself and it has no independent intelligence, but it is really fast. Once it has the right instructions, it works with lightning speed. It can add your column of numbers (even if it is twenty pages long) almost instantaneously. The program that allows you to compose letters and papers gives you a great deal of flexibility in editing. The ability to make extensive changes is something that was never possible with a type-writer without throwing away lots of paper and losing hours of work. Math and writing are just two small ways the computer can do wonderful things for us. Another great benefit of the computer is that with a connection to the Internet you are able to access information about almost anything on computers all over the world. There are places you can visit on the Internet that will help your children with their homework. You can book a vacation for the family.

When you've overcome your, shall we call it, e-phobia, you can pay your bills, make hotel and travel reservations, and control your finances electronically. Add the capability of email, and you can stay in touch with family members all over the world any time of day or night. All of these wonderful things happen when the computer system (your hardware) is given instructions (your software).

Figure 1c explains how the operating system works.

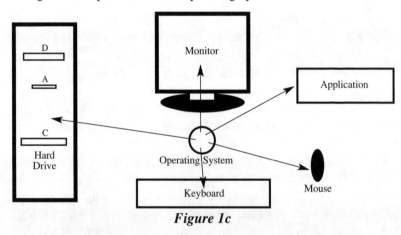

Figure 1c

The operating system is the systems software I talked about earlier. It is the software or program that tells the components of the computer system how to function. As you look at Figure1c, the operating system (software) resides on the computer's hard drive (C drive), and when you turn your computer on the operating system goes through a series of start-up routines. It checks to make sure all the components like the monitor, mouse, and keyboard are present and in working order. The start-up also establishes communication with your applications (i.e., word processing, accounting, games) and gets the system ready for work or play. Your application software is also residing on your hard drive in most cases. It is possible to have an application residing on a CD or a floppy disc, but this makes things run a bit slower because the operating system has to keep running back and forth between the drives to get the information it needs from the application. When the program sits on the hard drive it is more readily available and thus works faster.

The more you get into computing the more you will discover that fast is good. The advertisements you see for computers and auxiliary equipment (peripherals) are saturated with speed. "Buy me, I'm really, really fast!" the ads scream. While there is some truth to the "fast is good" theme, you will want to look carefully at what is necessary and what is nice to have, but not essential. I will take that up in the section on selecting and purchasing your computer.

Most of us will be using the Microsoft® Windows® operating system.[1] The current version of this software is Windows® 2000. Some computers are still using earlier versions called Windows® 98, Windows® 95, or even an older version called Windows® 3.0.*

Figure 1d

---

* Microsoft® Windows®, Windows® 2000, Windows®98, Windows® 95, and Windows® 3.0 are either registered trademarks of Microsoft Corporation in the United States and/or other countries.

Figure 1d is a picture (screen shot) of a monitor screen when the Microsoft Windows operating system first starts. Every computer will have a different screen depending on what programs are installed. Each little picture, usually called an icon, is a doorway to the program or application you want to use. In order to start the word processing program, all you need to do is move the arrow that is controlled by the mouse to the word processor window and double-click the left button of the mouse. This tells the operating system to get the word processing program and open it up so that you can type a letter or write a paper. The word processing program will open up in a window. In Figure 1e below, someone has clicked the word processor icon, and the program (here it is Microsoft Word) opens up in a window.

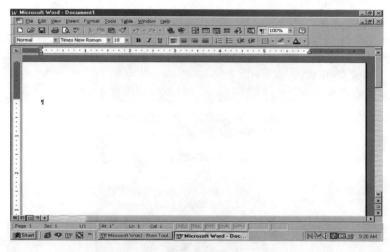

Figure 1e

The really neat thing is that you can open up more than one program and switch back and forth between the two. Your daughter who is in college, for instance, could open her checking account program and her word processing program. She could have the information from her checkbook available in one window as she composes a letter to you in the other window saying how desperately she needs more money.

Hang on! Here's your very first tech term. Memorize this to impress your computer-illiterate friends. When you open up two or more programs, each of them will open in its own window and you can switch back and forth between programs. You will learn quickly how to do this once you get your computer set up. Working with more than one program at the same time is called multitasking. One of the biggest advantages to an operating system such as Microsoft Windows is multitasking. You might tuck this term away to throw out in a nonchalant manner sometime, say, at a dinner party. Someone asks, "How's it going?" You reply, "Well, pretty good actually. I just upgraded my computer's operating system, and it has a wonderful multitasking capability!"

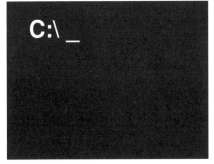

Figure 1f

The introduction of Microsoft Windows and the mouse was very good news for people who did not feel comfortable with the computer when it was controlled by the old DOS (disc operating system). The computer using the DOS system featured a screen (see Figure 1f) that was blank except for the C:\ or the "C" prompt. The C:\ was followed by an obnoxious cursor that seemed to impatiently blink away waiting for the user to type in instructions. The computer user had to type in instructions about where a program was located and then type a command to start the program. If the instructions were not typed in exactly as the computer needed, the program would not open and you would get an error message. If you wanted to work with more than one program, it was necessary to close one program and type in more commands to open up the next program.

The introduction of the Microsoft Windows operating system was wonderful. All a person had to do was click a window and a program started up.

When you sit down to interact with a computer, you are interfacing with the computer. The old DOS way of interfacing was to type in commands. The new way is to click an icon (picture). Much easier. Here's your second tech term. The Microsoft Windows method of interfacing with a computer is through a graphical user interface or GUI (pronounced "gooey"). Each program represented on your screen has its own graphic or icon. You begin a program by interfacing with the computer through these graphics.

There are other operating systems (such as DOS—disc operating system, and OS/2—operating system two, which was developed by IBM and Linux, another software company), though Microsoft Windows is the dominant operating system in the PC world today.

Peripherals

THE TRIMMINGS: "WHAT ELSE WOULD YOU LIKE?"

One of the things you will want to do before you journey out to buy your computer is to decide exactly what you want to do with it. For instance, if you just want to type a few letters, send and receive email, and surf the Web once in a while, then go out and get the $799 machine. If you plan to open a small business, design and deploy a Web site, get a camera and save family photo albums on your computer, you will want to buy the $2,999 model.

Here are a few of the extras (peripherals) you can choose from. When you have gone through the list, you can make use of the chart that follows to help you decide which computer will work best for you.

Printer

Although you can work on your computer and surf the Internet without a printer, you should probably consider a printer a necessary peripheral. Even if you simply want to write letters and papers, you will need a printer.

Printers cost anywhere from less than $100 up to $600.

There are three basic types of printers available. The dot matrix printer works by means of a set of pins striking a ribbon that transfers the dots to the paper. Most home users do not use these because of the lesser quality of print, especially for graphics. Businesses that use computers to fill in multiple-part forms have to use a dot matrix printer because the other types will not work for this function. The second, and most popular type of printer, is the ink-jet or bubble jet printer, which works by forcing little drops of ink from a cartridge onto the paper. The ink dries almost instantly and the quality is good. Ink-jet printers will cost from just under $100 to $400 for a very nice quality printer that will work well with photographs. The third, and highest quality type of printer, is the laser printer. A black-and-white laser printer costs anywhere from $300 to $600. Color laser printers are much more expensive, beginning at approximately $1,500.

Scanner

Most people do not need a scanner for home use. But a scanner for the church is very useful. A scanner can copy a page of text or photos directly into your computer. Photographs of a youth group meeting or church picnic could be scanned for use in a church newsletter.

Three different types of scanners have been in use over the past few years. One is the handheld scanner, which is passed over a page to capture the text or graphic. It looks a bit like the scanner department stores use to read the bar codes on packages. The second type of scanner is a page scanner. This works by inserting a page into the scanner, capturing the image as the page passes through. A third type of scanner is the flatbed scanner. It looks and works more like a copy machine. Place a page, photograph, or book on the scanner and, with a method that is much like a copier, scan it into a computer file.

In previous years the primary consideration in choosing a scanner was economic. The handheld scanner was the least expensive, the page scanner more expensive, and the flatbed the most expensive. Because of a significant drop in prices, a flatbed scanner is well within the reach of most users at less than $100 for the least expensive. The price of the scanner increases in direct proportion to its ability to scan graphic images. The higher the quality of the image you desire, the more the cost of the scanner. You should be able to purchase a scanner for about $200 that will do a nice job with images.

Note: One issue you will need to deal with when purchasing peripheral equipment is knowing how to connect that equipment to your computer. If you look back at Figure 1c, the operating system will need to talk to your scanner (or other peripheral) in order to make it work with everything else. You will use a cord to plug the scanner into the back of the box that holds the computer's brain. There are two ways to plug the scanner into the box. One cord comes with a plug that fits into a parallel port. The other comes with a cord that plugs into a USB port.

Is there a difference? Yes. USB stands for "universal serial bus." It is a newer type of connection that has become common in the past couple of years. The old parallel port needed an extra program to tell the computer what piece of equipment was attached. This program sometimes needed the computer operator to tell the program what kinds of information the computer needed in order to make the equipment work. Sometimes there would be difficulty when two or more peripherals were going to use a parallel port and the computer would sit there like a dummy, not knowing what to do.

Wouldn't it be great if the computer's operating system could do all that communication without you and I having to go through all the headache of setting up each new piece of equipment? That was the idea behind USB. When you plug your scanner in, the operating system knows what is there and knows how to tell the computer what to do with it. One of the questions I always have when buying equipment such as a scanner is, "Does it have a USB connection?"

Digital Camera

A digital camera will allow you to take photographs and load them directly onto your computer. Some cameras come with a program that will allow you to transfer the photographic image to your computer (that is, download the picture or file). A few cameras like the Sony Mavica family will store the picture on a 3.5" floppy disc that you can put directly into your computer's floppy drive.

There are several low-priced digital cameras available, but as of this writing there are no inexpensive ($200 or less) digital cameras that can get the image quality of a similarly priced film-based camera. If you want a digital camera for good-quality family photos, plan to spend at least $400 and up.

A digital camera, such as the Sony Mavica series, is a handy peripheral to have if you want graphics for the Internet. These cameras begin at about $500. However, for most users, a lower-priced scanner will adequately accomplish the task of producing graphics for Internet use.

Joystick

A joystick is essential for those who plan to play a lot of games with their computers. Although most games can be played with a mouse, the joystick makes it easier and faster. The key question for parents is whether to turn the computer into a video arcade. If you are making a purchasing decision with your children, it could be wise to hold off on buying the joystick until the educational aims of your purchase are in place. But if you have your heart set on getting a flight simulator for your computer, you will need a joystick, which you can get for about $50.

ZIP Drive

A ZIP drive is a storage device that holds a lot of data. It comes in either 100 or 250 MB models. One 250 MB disc will hold as much data as about 170 floppy discs. This drive can be especially important for backing up programs and files on your computer that you do not want to lose. You have probably heard people say something like, "My computer crashed!" When a serious crash occurs, you can lose lots of work and important files. A ZIP drive can help by providing enough space to back up files you are especially

concerned about protecting. ZIP discs also provide a way to trans-
port lots of information from one place to another. If you plan to
work with a lot of graphics, you might consider a ZIP drive to store
those memory-hogging photographs and other images. Is a ZIP
drive essential? No. However, lots of extra storage for a price of
about $140 could be helpful. *Unless* you decide on a CD-RW drive
instead of a plain old CD drive. CD-RW drives have become inexpensive and ZIP drive technology will become less popular.

CD-RW

A CD-RW (Compact Disc–Rewritable) is very similar to the CD-
ROM drive I described above. The difference is that with a CD-RW
drive you can write information on the compact disc as well as read
the disc. Since a CD holds so much information (almost the equivalent of 450 floppy discs), it can be used to store photographs and
other large files. This would save space on your hard drive. The
ability to create your own CDs would be valuable for those who
have large amounts of information they would like to pass on to others.

You can purchase a computer with a CD-RW by adding just over
$100 to the cost of the computer. Since a CD-RW drive will read the
disc as well as write on it, this would take the place of a simple CD-
ROM. If you were to include a CD-RW drive on your computer, you
would not need the ZIP drive for extra storage.

Surge Protector

A surge protector will help protect your computer from power
surges. It is inexpensive insurance. Any computer store or office
supply store can help you find the proper surge protector for your
needs. The surge protector has a fuse that will stop the current to
your computer if a power surge (spike) occurs. If you will be using
a telephone line to link your computer's modem to the Internet, then
you should get a surge protector that has a telephone jack.

The surge protector might not protect your computer during electrical storms. The only way to ensure your computer doesn't get

fried in the event of a lightning strike is to unplug both computer and modem during a storm.

* * *

That's it! There are tons of bells and whistles you can buy for your computer, but most of them are not things you need. As time goes on you will develop the ability to tell what is necessary and what is nice but not necessary.

Configuring Your Computer

That wasn't so bad was it? You are just about ready to go out and purchase your computer with a sense of confidence. Go through the chart on page 38 to help decide which computer would be best for your needs. (You will hear this process called "configuring your computer.") Some of the most common tasks in computing are listed with an "X" in column A, B, or C, which suggests the minimum computer system configuration you should consider. Computer programs come in boxes that usually list the system requirements or minimum suggested by the creator of the program.

Hint: Don't believe it! The requirements suggested by the creators of the program are absolute, bottom-of-the-barrel suggestions. They want everyone to buy their product, so they aim at the minimum computer configuration it will take to make their program work. To be sure, the program will work on minimums, but this is rather like saying it is *possible* to count the grains of sand in a gallon jar. The fact is, however, that you would not really want to spend time actually doing the counting. Personally, I've never been happy with a program unless I have at least double the requirements listed on the box. My chart is based on the assumption that you want your programs to work with decent speed.

TASK*	A	B	C
Word Processing (letters, term papers, essays, church newsletter)	X		
Personal Accounting (checkbook, do your taxes)	X		
Email	X		
Use the Internet	X		
Create a Web Site	X		
Create a Large Web Site (with lots of graphics)		X	
Create a *Really* Large Web Site (with lots of graphics and interactivity)			X
Photography (take and store photographs, build a family photo album)		X	
Church Management (membership, financial, outreach information)		X	
Create Brochures		X	
Play Video Games (maybe lots of *big* games)		X	X
Create a Full-Featured Interactive Web Site			X
Create Video Files and Movies			X

*If you have any doubt as to whether you will want to do a bit more, it is much easier to move up a notch now than to go through an upgrade or a new purchase.

A	B	C
500 MHz Processor** (see next section about drive processors), 64 MB RAM, CD-ROM, 6.5 GB Hard Drive, Any Ink-Jet Printer	700 MHz Processor, 128 MB RAM, CD-ROM, 10 GB Hard Drive, Mid-Level Ink-Jet Printer, Digital Camera (if doing photos)	1000 MHz Processor, 256 MB RAM, 15 GB Drive (and above), Higher-Level Ink-Jet Printer, Scanner (or Digital Camera?)

Figure 1g

A Note About Processors

The most popular processors that you will see listed in computer ads are AMD (a competitor to the popular, most widely used Intel processors), the Celeron (made by Intel), and the Pentium. The Pentium chip is the most popular processor, having gone through four generations. If you are seeking the system listed as "A," any of the processors will work well. The AMD and Celeron chips are a bit less expensive. If you are seeking the system I've called "C," it will serve you well to stick with the Pentium III and Pentium 4 (games also work best on these processors). The specifications in the chart on page 36 will change, and you will want to check the companion Web site (*www.newtools-online*) for updates. The selection process, however, will remain the same.

Where to Purchase Your Computer

Armed with information on what you need in a computer, you set out to make the purchase. Computers are available from a large number of suppliers, and most people obtain their computers from one of three places: You can buy through (1) a mail-order/Internet-based company, (2) a department/office supply store, or (3) a local computer builder.

1. Find a magazine about computers and you can find mail-order and Web-based companies that sell computers. For your first computer purchase, it would be a good idea to avoid the mail-order houses that simply act as a reseller or distributor for other companies. Gateway and Dell are two excellent companies with a reputation for quality and good customer service. With either company, you can order by phone with your credit card, configure your computer the way you want it, and have it in about ten days. As of this writing, for instance, Gateway had a remanufactured computer with a one-year limited warranty that could very nicely handle the tasks of our "System A" for $699. Dell had a similar system for $659. The world of computer pricing changes fast, but usually in favor of the consumer.

2. A second way to buy your computer is to look at the big

department and office supply stores. Best Buy, Circuit City, Staples, and OfficeMax are just a few of the stores that carry a large supply of computers. One of the advantages of this kind of purchase is that these large stores offer significant discounts and usually have a large inventory. Since the salespersons are not invested in any one particular manufacturer, they are willing to give fairly objective advice. Most stores will throw in a printer or a scanner or some other peripheral to sweeten the deal. If you do purchase a system that comes with a printer, be sure it will give the kind of quality you need. If you need what I defined as a "System C," for instance, a $99 printer will not be sufficient.

One of the advantages of buying from these larger stores is that you can take the system home in a box and be computing that evening. The systems come with the software loaded and ready to go. When you plug the components into the box, the box into your surge protector (don't forget this piece), and the surge protector into the wall, turn on the power switch and you will be in business!

3. Another way to go in your first purchase is to choose a local person who builds computers. These persons assemble the computer with parts they purchase and are able to put together the system you want. Most of the local people who build computers for a living give excellent customer service since they are dependent upon the goodwill of the people of the community. The number one advantage with a local purchase is the availability of advice from your local builder and a place to take your computer in the event of a problem. *Be sure* to check around with a few folks who have done business with the person you are considering. While most are very good, you do need to know a merchant's track record. When you buy from John Doe in your hometown, the product is as good as John Doe and his name. When you buy from Gateway or Dell, you have a corporation standing behind the product.

Beware of the Free Lunch

There is one strong caution you should consider. Beware of all the ads that promise a free computer or give you a large rebate if you sign up with a particular Internet service. One service, for instance, was offering large rebates for people who signed up for as much as three years of Internet service with them. With the discount, you could purchase a new computer for anywhere from $0 to $199. The problem is that technology is changing so fast that three years from now might as well be three light-years. You will likely be able to use cable for Internet access, which is twenty to thirty times faster than phone lines. Prices will drop for every kind of connection as competition grows and the Internet industry continues to expand.

If I offered you a free car in return for a legally binding agreement that you would buy your gas from me for the rest of your life, would you take it? Or might you want to know things like, How much will the gas cost? Will the price keep rising? Will gas be obsolete in a few years? When you buy your computer, take all the discounts and rebates you can get, but don't accept any "free lunches." One of my favorite things to do is to lodge a complaint with the stores (and it's most of them) when I see the signs that scream:

"Super Duper Computer System—$100.00!!"

[$799–$100 Manufacturer's Discount–$100 Instant Store Discount–$499 Internet Service Provider Discount (with 3-year contract for Internet service) = $100]

Tell the clerk, "No thanks, I'll buy my own lunch." Go ahead and pay the $599, take the $200 in discounts, save a bundle on your Internet service, and get better service in the bargain.

There is another not-so-free freebie. The pastor and church secretary should beware of companies that call and offer to provide a free Web site for the church. They tell you they will design and publish a Web site at no cost. All they need is a few details and your authorization to build the site. One church secretary informed her pastor, "It sounded good to me and everyone needs a Web site, so I told them to go ahead." It took three months to get the contract canceled. It turned out that the site design was free and the publishing of the site was free, but there was a $29.95 monthly hosting fee that was automatically added to the church's monthly phone bill. If you want a fast and easy way to have a church Web site that is *really* free, I will show you how to do that in chapter 7.

Launch Time

Your computer is finally put together, plugged in, and ready to go. Turn on the power, fasten your seat belt, and get ready for your launch into cyberspace. This is going to be great!

Chapter Two

Really, Really Basic Internet Stuff

Oops!

I should have said you are *almost* ready to launch into cyber-space. There are a few things about accessing the Internet and getting around on the Web that we need to look at. Unless, of course you might want to:

Skip This Chapter?

If you are familiar with the Internet from using a friend's computer, or perhaps from surfing at work (on your lunch hour, of course), or if you have done some Internet browsing at the local library, go to the Appendix and try Skip Quiz #2. From there you can decide whether you want to skip or skim this chapter. Otherwise this chapter will help you prepare to use the Internet.

Understanding the Internet

In just a short time, you will be able to talk Web talk with your friends. It is not all that mysterious. Once you become acquainted with a few technical terms, you will be comfortable with the world of the Internet. As you have already discovered, this world is filled with acronyms like *RAM, ROM,* and the like.

To get started: The World Wide Web, the Web, or the Internet all refer to the same thing. The Internet was originally intended to link computers at a university to one another and later to computers at other universities; thus a network or Internet. Military and business communities were also in on early development of the Internet because they saw potential for military and commercial use. Obviously, the growth of the Internet has exploded beyond the wildest imaginings of the most visionary of the early Internet pioneers. Computers from universities, commercial corporations, governments, and the family that grows corn out in the middle of Iowa can talk to one another. A farmer in France can communicate with the farmer in Iowa instantly.

It is possible for me to put a fence around my computer and give a key to only those people I want to enter my computer or Web site. That's called security, but some really smart (and even not so smart) people can figure a way under or through the fence. They hack their way into my computer anyway. You know what we call them, right? Hackers. You have heard news reports about these hackers and the frenzy they can cause. The plus side of all these security issues is that the safety and security of using the Internet improve each time a security incident is reported or a scam perpetrated.

Hacking is the electronic equivalent of breaking and entering. When robbers break into a store or force their way into someone's house, there are laws that allow these thieves to be convicted and fined or put in jail. One indicator that the Internet world moves at a fast pace is the fact that the laws are playing catch-up with electronic crime. The good news is that electronic thieves are not really interested in the computer at your home. For those issues you should be concerned about, I will discuss Internet safety for your family in chapter 5.

The number of Web sites available on the Internet has exploded since 1993. At the end of 1993, the number of Web site hosts was 623. As of July 1, 2001, the number was estimated at over 31 million.[1] Actually, the number of individual Web sites is larger because a Web site host will usually contain more than one Web site. Web sites are now being added to the World Wide Web at the rate of thousands per day. Various resources put the number higher or lower and there is no accurate way to say for sure, but there is one thing you can count on. The Internet is mind-boggling both in size and in impact on our culture.

The Internet isn't sitting in any one place and there is no one agency that regulates the Internet. It, like the spider's web, runs here and there and is loosely held together by the individual strands. If one strand breaks, the web still hangs together in some fashion and the spider just keeps spinning her web.

So, welcome to the World Wide Web or the Internet. The Internet is no longer a phenomenon, but a genuine revolution in our contemporary world. We have yet to see exactly how extensive this revolution will be, but it is certain we in the church need to be attentive to something that will have an impact on all of our members in the coming years.

How Do I Connect to the Internet?

In order to connect to the Internet, you need a modem that is a part of your computer. A regular telephone cord plugs into the modem and to a telephone jack. When you talk to someone on the phone, the telephone lines carry your voice as data. This same line can carry other kinds of data, such as a fax. You have probably dialed a phone number at one time or another and heard a terrible screeching noise on the other end. You know by the terrible sound that you have connected with a fax machine. You and the fax machine are exchanging data, but neither of you understands the other's data. With the Internet, your computer exchanges data with another computer called a server.

The idea of a computer server is not all that different from a restaurant server. Restaurant servers are the people who bring your food and drinks. You are the client or customer. Voilà! That's also how it works with the exchange of data between computers. Your computer is the client computer, and the computer you connect to is the server that serves up the information you are seeking.

In order to connect to the Internet, you need an Internet service provider, or ISP. You use your computer to dial up your ISP and the

ISP's computer, or server, will link you to the Internet. It is as though the Internet is a huge interstate highway that leads all over the world, and your ISP is the on-ramp you use to get on the highway.

AOL, AT&T, and other companies are Internet service providers, but they are very large and have so many customers you will sometimes get a busy signal when you try to connect. When you have trouble getting connected or have other problems with your Internet access, it will be difficult to find a human being to talk to in those large companies. A local ISP offers technical support you cannot get with the large corporations. There are many places, especially in small towns, where you may have to make a long-distance call to connect to your ISP. In this instance there is no way around the phone charges and you will need to pay more attention to the time spent online. Fortunately, there are more ISPs with local phone numbers that offer service. One advantage to a company like AOL is that you can obtain a CD that can be put into your CD drive. The program will automatically begin to run, and by following the directions on your monitor you will soon be connected and ready to surf. Some people sign up with AOL or EarthLink (another ISP) for the free trial and use the trial period to learn their way around the Internet. Once they learn their way around and reach a degree of comfort with the process of using the Internet and email, they switch to a local ISP. If you choose to do this, *be sure* to write down all information you see during the sign-up about canceling your service. When it comes time to cancel at the end of your trial, you may have difficulty retrieving this information.

My opinion is that the best way to get connected to the Internet is to find a local ISP. (Look in the Yellow Pages under "computers" or "Internet.") Talk to any friends who use the Internet. As with any company, there are good ISPs and not-so-good ISPs. Most of them are quite willing to help you get through the process of setting up your computer to connect to the Internet.

Once you are on the highway, you need to know where to go. For instance, if you got in your car and drove to Texas looking for your friend Jimmy Robinson, you would have to have an exact place to go. It wouldn't help much if you drove until you saw a sign saying "Welcome to Texas," stopped the first person you encountered, and said that you were looking for Jimmy Robinson. You need a specific address in order to find Jimmy. It is the same idea with the Internet. You need to have an exact address of where you want data to come from. This is called a URL (uniform resource locator). The URL is the exact Internet address for the data or Web site you want to visit. If the address is not exact, you will not get to your destination. A comma, a period, or a slash out of place very quickly demonstrates the fact that the browser's insistence on a correct URL is unforgiving.

Going to the wrong address can be a big problem. Perhaps you have seen one of those news reports about a city demolition crew that has mistakenly demolished the wrong building. There was an incident in a large midwestern city in which a condemned house was scheduled for demolition. A man returned home from work one day and to his horror found that his house had been turned into a pile of toothpicks. The demolition crew had made a tiny little error. The address of the condemned house was off by only one digit and the home across from the condemned house was demolished. Fortunately for you, nothing so disastrous as this will happen if you type in an incorrect Internet address, but you can get an irritating message along the lines of, "Web Site Not Found."

Let's assume you contract with a local ISP and get your computer connected to the Internet. What happens next?

Your computer needs a software program called a browser to show you the Web pages that are available on the Internet. What is a browser? The term *browser* does indeed come from a familiar phrase we've all used in the department stores. A clerk comes to ask if you need help and you reply, "No, thank you, just browsing." When you get connected to the Internet and want to do some browsing (that is, visit Web sites), you will need a browser. When you search the Internet, the browser looks at documents on other computers and then tells your computer how to display what it sees. The browser sees code and displays text and pictures. For instance, your browser will see something like this:

```
<html>
<head>
<meta http-equiv="Content-Language" content="en-us">
<meta http-equiv="Content-Type" content="text/html;
charset=windows-1252">
<title>New Page 1</title>
</head>
<body>
<p><font face="Arial" size="3"><b>This is a Web
page.</b></font></p>
<p><font face="Arial" size="3"><b>This is a picture on a
Web page:</b></font></p>
<p><img border="0"
src="file:///c:/windows/TEMP/FrontPageTempDir/pe03254_.
wmf" width="147" height="133"></p>
</body>
</html>
```

And show you this:

This is a Web page.
This is a picture on a Web page:

Your browser tells the code, which is called HTML (hypertext markup language), what to display. Microsoft Internet Explorer®[2] is one browser. Netscape® is another.* They do see things a little bit differently, but they work pretty well with most Web sites. Between

---

* Netscape and the Netscape N and Ship's Wheel logos are registered trademarks of Netscape Communications Corporation in the U.S. and other countries.

the two they represent 98 percent of all browsers used in the world. Both browsers are updated regularly. Most computers have a browser installed as part of the software. A free copy of either browser can be downloaded from the companies' respective Web sites.

Other Ways to Connect: Cable, DSL, Direct Web

The majority of people who use the Internet are dialup or tele-phone line–based customers using their regular phone lines. The cost for unlimited access (meaning you can get on the Internet and stay there for as long as you like) runs approximately $20 a month. When you want to access the Internet you will click on a dialup icon and wait while the computer's modem makes those funny little fax machine–like noises and establishes a connection.

There are a couple of issues you will need to deal with when you first connect. Have you ever tried to call a friend whose teenager had a new computer with Internet access? The telephone line was busy most of the time. When you are connected, or online, your tele-phone line is busy. There are two ways to correct this: (1) Get a sec-ond telephone line just for your computer, or (2) get voice mail (a less expensive way to go). Voice mail will at least take messages while your line is busy.

Another way to connect to the Internet is through cable. This is the same type of cable used in cable television. If you already have cable television, cable access to the Internet may be available in your area. The great advantage to cable access is that once you have cable access you are connected all the time, and you do not have to dial a number to initiate the connection. Cable access is also much faster than dialup, and you will spend much less time waiting for Web sites to download. Compare dialup access and cable access to plastic pipes. It will take much longer for an amount of water to travel through a 1/4" pipe than through a 12" pipe. The same applies to these Internet con-nections. Cable can carry a huge amount of data more quickly com-pared to your telephone line and modem setup. Cable costs about twice as much as dialup, but the price is likely to drop as competition for alternative means of access develops. With cable access there is no need for a second telephone line. The economic difference between dialup and cable access can be offset when two or more people in your home use the Internet for business or homework and talk of a second computer begins to surface. Faster download time from the Internet translates to less time per person required at the computer.

Yet another means of accessing the Internet is through DSL (digital subscriber lines), which is available in many areas through your local telephone company. The service is generally offered through your local ISP. DSL is also very fast and the price is approximately the same as for cable access.

A new direction in Internet technology is the increasing use of wireless access. Wireless means that the data is transmitted through the atmosphere much like a TV signal. Your television signal can come to you through the atmosphere and can be picked up by an antenna or it can come through cable. The technology is now available to transmit Internet data that can be picked up by a dish much like those used by companies like DirecTV. Wireless transmission of Internet data will need more time to gain popularity and reliability, but many see the future of the Internet in wireless access. The one area where wireless technology is growing rapidly is in the use of Internet data with the cell phone. If you think talking on a cell phone while driving is dangerous, wait until growing numbers of people are accessing their stock quotes and downloading email by means of wireless Internet!

For now, most of us will use dialup or cable with some using DSL. In the local church, cable and DSL are worth exploring. Cable access would mean eliminating the need for a second phone line and utilizing improved Internet access speed for educational and research uses.

Using the Internet: Searching, Email, Newsgroups, and Chat

SEARCHING

There are a number of ways to use the Internet in communicating around the globe. The most obvious, of course, is the ability to visit Web sites without the encumbrance of geographical boundaries. The problem is how to navigate the mountains of material available. Students have reported spending countless hours surfing the Net and coming up empty-handed in terms of substantive material for their class work.

Imagine walking into the largest library in the world without having a clue as to where to look for something you needed. What if there were no card catalogs, no resource listings, and no librarian who could answer your questions, only endless stacks of books, journals, and magazines? It would be overwhelming to the point that you might be tempted to skip using the library.

The search engine was invented as an answer to all this confusion. A search engine is an Internet-based librarian of sorts. You type a word into the search engine's search box, press Enter on your keyboard, and the search engine will list all the places you can visit on the Web that relate to your term.

When the search is completed, you will have a list of sites that relate to your word (search term). The Web sites are listed as underlined text. When you move your cursor (using the mouse) over one of these sites marked with underlined text, your cursor will change from an arrow shape like this, ⌂, to a finger shape like this, ⌐. When the cursor changes, you can click the left button on your mouse and your browser will take you to the site. The underlined text is called a hyperlink. It causes your browser to jump to another Web site. You will soon discover that there is a bit of a learning curve in using search engines. The term *school,* for instance, returned 3,151 possible sites to visit in one search engine. And this is just one of about 650 search engines and directories worldwide. The search engine solution has become almost as confusing as the Web was before search engines.

There are, however, a few search engines that outrank the others. I suggest limiting your initial work with search engines to four or five among those listed on the companion Web site. To get you started, I recommend the search engine at *www.google.com*. Most search engines have a tutorial or information on how to perform effective searches. They are well worth the time it will take to learn the ins and outs of search engines. This is something like having the librarian explain to you how the library is set up and what to look for.

EMAIL

Email stands for electronic mail. Email is a great way to communicate with others. It is fast, inexpensive, and easy to learn. When you sign up for an account with an ISP, you will be asked to choose an email name. The format will be the name you choose followed by the name of your ISP. The ISP acts as your post office, and your email account is referred to as your mailbox. If your ISP is named mytown.com, for instance, your mailbox will be at mytown.com (@mytown.com). That's the post office. In order for email to arrive at your mailbox, you will provide the name you want to use just before the name of the post office (i.e., *mary@mytown.com*). If there is already a Mary at your post office, you will be asked to choose another name. You can use any combination of letters and numbers in your email address. You could use your birthday, age, or high school class year and be *mary21@mytown.com.*

The program you use to create email (your email client) comes with your browser. Microsoft Internet Explorer comes with an email client called Outlook Express®.* Netscape provides a client called WebMail. Both are easy to learn. Services like AOL, EarthLink, and AT&T all provide their own email clients. If you choose to use a local ISP, you can usually ask them to help you get your email program set up at the same time you set up your Internet connection.

NEWSGROUPS

Newsgroups are like discussion groups, except they are not conducted in real time as chat groups are. Someone will send a message, an opinion, or an essay to a newsgroup (post a message), and everyone who signs up for that newsgroup can read the message and respond if they wish. One of the nice things about newsgroups is

---

* Microsoft Outlook Express® is either a registered trademark or trademark of Microsoft Corporation in the United States and/or other countries.

that they are asynchronous. You can participate at your own leisure and at whatever time you wish. It's a bit like reading messages on a message board at the school or club. With *this* message board you can post your own messages in response.

There are literally thousands of newsgroups and thousands of people who spend a lot of time using newsgroups as personal soapboxes. Both Microsoft Outlook Express and Netscape WebMail have newsgroup functions. If you have time and energy for newsgroups, I recommend visiting the Web site *www.liszt.com* and reading through all the groups listed. You can visit various newsgroups and sign up to receive messages from those you wish to participate in.

CHAT

Chat rooms on the Internet are places where you can visit and participate in real-time conversations. This is an area that has received a lot of discussion concerning the dangers of the Internet for children. I will discuss Internet safety and family-friendly Internet usage in the next chapter.

Beginning Your Journey

When you have finally set up your computer and have arranged for access to the Internet, you will want to begin your journey by visiting a few Web sites and using a search engine to find information you are looking for. One of the most helpful sites on the Internet for finding information is about.com (*www.about.com*). This site offers information on absolutely everything you can imagine. It also includes links for further exploration of your topic. A good place to begin is to put the term *Internet surfing* in the search box at about.com. The result will give further information for family-safe surfing and help you gain discernment as you begin your journey on the information superhighway.

The easiest way to learn the ins and outs of the Internet is to spend time surfing and working with the search engines.

Part Two
PRELIMINARIES

Once the church and increasing numbers of the congregation are connected, what comes next? In this section I do a bit of theological reflection on the impact of technology on the church, our families, and our ministry. What are the roles of pastors, Christian educators, and lay leaders in the current environment? How can Christian parents offer guidance to children who frequently know more than their parents do about technology?

Chapter Three

Would Jesus Carry a Pager?

Jesus and the Meaning of Being Connected: The Master's Model

One of the foundation principles of the Christian faith is community. Jesus was bound to his disciples and his disciples to one another by a very powerful bond of love. "As I have loved you, so you must love one another," he commanded (John 13:34 NIV). This band of followers lived together, traveled together, and in their first attempts at ministry, worked in pairs as they took the good news to their world.

When that very first mission trip was over, the group gathered to debrief. Jesus called his disciples together for frequent learning (usually on-the-job type training), and took them on retreats. The Gospel of Mark tells of one of those times: "Because so many people were coming and going that they did not even have a chance to eat, he said to them, 'Come with me by yourselves to a quiet place and get some rest' " (Mark 6:31 NIV).

Being together and being in touch were essential to the growth and development of those who would eventually bear responsibility for bringing the good news of Jesus Christ to the rest of the world.

When the time came, Jesus bade his followers farewell and gave them two very important things:

1. He gave them specific instructions about the work they were to do.

> Then Jesus came to them and said, "All authority in heaven and on earth has been given to me. Therefore go and make disciples of all nations, baptizing them in the name of the Father and of the Son and of the Holy Spirit, and teaching them to obey everything I have commanded you. And surely I am with you always, to the very end of the age." (Matthew 28:18-20 NIV)

2. He gave them a promise that they would receive power to get the job done.

> You will receive power when the Holy Spirit comes on you; and you will be my witnesses in Jerusalem, and in all Judea and Samaria, and to the ends of the earth. (Acts 1:8)

In short, Jesus wanted his followers to have clear instructions about their purpose and the resources to carry out that purpose.

A thought comes to mind. Wouldn't it have been wonderful if the earliest followers of Jesus could have stayed in touch with one another by email? Imagine Peter and Paul having a technologically enabled way to talk about the interaction between Jewish and gentile believers before things got out of hand. Or what it might have meant for the apostle Paul and those struggling early churches if he could have communicated with them by means of wireless email while he was in prison.

Remember that huge conflict in the Galatian church? It seems some people came to town after Paul's time of ministry and were well on the way to destroying the meaning of grace. Their basic thrust was that gentiles had to become Jews and keep all the Jewish laws in order to be Christians. By the time Paul was able to get his letter to the church, things were almost out of control. If only he had the ability to have a cyberchat with those new Christians!

Jesus appointed seventy-two of his followers and sent them two by two as advance teams to every town and place where he was about to go. "He told them, 'The harvest is plentiful, but the workers are few. Ask the Lord of the harvest, therefore, to send out workers into his harvest field. Go! I am sending you out like lambs among wolves'" (Luke 10:2-3 NIV). If this injunction to ministry were given in our time, I am convinced that someone would ask something along the line of, "Lord, do you have a pager where you can be reached if things get really tough?"

The close bond between Jesus and his disciples raises a question. If such things had been available at the time, would Jesus have carried a pager? When the threat of separation from Jesus brought anxiety to the Twelve, Jesus promised, "I will not leave you as orphans; I will come to you" (John 14:18 NIV). Along with his final instructions, he said, "I am with you always, to the end of the age" (Matthew 28:20).

Would Jesus' commitment to continue with his disciples have included carrying a pager, a cell phone, and a laptop?

Obviously I say this tongue in cheek, but increasing numbers of pastors are carrying cell phones and pagers. Each day finds more clergy using email to stay in touch with parishioners. One pastor commented, "I use email in counseling and find some people who are reluctant to talk in person find it easier to share their lives through email." There is a sense in which all these tools make pastors increasingly available for ministry. Computer and software companies who desire to get an edge in their market advertise "24-7" support. You can reach them for service twenty-four hours a day, seven days a week, holidays included. Isn't it a wonderful thing that those of us in ministry as pastors or laypeople can be available to others on a 24-7 basis?

Or is it?

Jesus' incarnational presence in our world—the word become flesh—reflects God's always and forever care for us. "His eye is on the sparrow," the old song says. God has the hairs on our head all numbered. There is never a time when God is unaware of us or inattentive to our needs. When Jesus spoke of anxiety in our lives, he said, "Look at the birds of the air; they do not sow or reap or store away in barns, and yet your heavenly Father feeds them. Are you not much more valuable than they?" (Matthew 6:26 NIV).

Jesus made the ultimate commitment of love to his disciples and asked them to have that same love and commitment toward one another and the lost world he would commission them to reach. On the surface, this would seem to translate into pager-carrying, cell phone–using, emailing pastors and lay leaders.

However, it is important to be aware of an essential dynamic in Jesus' relationship with his disciples and with a world filled with urgent needs. Jesus had a lively and instructive balance between being together *with* and being apart *from* his disciples and the crowds. Remember the time Jesus got up early, before the crack of dawn, and slipped off for a time of prayer and renewal? The previous day had been one of those never-ending, energy-draining days of ministry. It was time for Jesus to have some time alone in prayer, but you can almost hear the disciples' surprise that he would leave them without so much as a note as to where he could be reached.

> Very early in the morning, while it was still dark, Jesus got up, left the house and went off to a solitary place, where he prayed. Simon and his companions went to look for him, and when they found him, they exclaimed: "Everyone is looking for you!"
>
> Jesus replied, "Let us go somewhere else—to the nearby villages—so I can preach there also. That is why I have come." (Mark 1:35-38 NIV)

Here's a key principle that holds special significance in a time when technological tools can make us available on a 24-7 basis. *If we are not available to God, we cannot truly be available to those we minister to.* Jesus not only knew he had to take time away from the crowd and from his disciples, he knew it was time to move on to other villages where good news was needed.

Spiritual/Theological Reflections on Technology

Technology as Servant

There is a danger that accompanies the use of technological tools. In the fields of computing and the Internet, the term *ubiquitous* has become a buzzword. According to *The American Heritage*

Dictionary of the English Language, 4th Edition, one of the meanings of the word is "omnipresent." Ubiquitous computing and Internet means that you can use your computer and other tools (or toys) everywhere, all the time. It should give us pause and induce caution to realize that we are speaking of technological tools in terms that have traditionally been reserved for the Lord God. Omnipresence is a quality of God. Unlike your ubiquitous cell phone, God's batteries will not die on you.

When we carry cell phones or pagers, the expectation is that we are available at all times. For pastors and other church leaders, there is already a temptation toward a messianic complex. The availability of tools that give the sense of always being available can lead to unhealthy expectations on the part of those to whom we minister. If we are not careful, these tools can exacerbate our vulnerability to the messianic complex.

Jesus made extensive use of images in the world around him. The lilies of the field that "neither toil nor spin," the birds of the air that "neither sow nor reap nor gather into barns" are clothed gloriously and fed abundantly reflecting the sovereign care of God. He used parables and imagination to teach essential concepts about the nature and character of God. As a heartbroken father longs for the return of a wayward son, so God longs for the return of all persons to his loving embrace. Graphic images and illustrative stories were powerful tools in the Master's teaching style. We can reasonably conclude that Jesus would use all available tools to bring the good news of God's love and care. If he were teaching in our time, he would more than likely use the tools our young people are using.

Technology provides us with terrific new tools for ministry. These tools are not the main point, but are intended to serve the main point, namely our life together in the family of faith. Technology is a wonderful servant, but it is also a terrible master. Technology in the service of ministry will give us new ways to communicate, to reach out, and even to worship. The crucial point is ministry. If technological resources are used simply to produce a tech show or to entertain ourselves, we simply build another form of the golden calf.

Angela Garber has observed, "New technology can simplify the creation and production process and help you achieve impressive looking results, but don't let that technology get in the way of the message. If you've put together a laser light show with a rock-and-roll soundtrack, you've probably let technology overwhelm the presentation. But whether you're using PowerPoint, Web-conference tools, or electronic whiteboards, always keep your message and audience in mind. Then think about the best way to get that message across."[1]

Who is Angela Garber? You might think she is a Christian education leader who is concerned that the good news not take a backseat to technology. Actually, she is a staff writer for *Small Business Computing,* a magazine dedicated to technology for the small-business market. Her concern in allowing the essential message of any presentation to remain center stage while supported by technology applies especially well for the use of technology in ministry.

Can "Cyberchurch" Provide or Replace Community?

There are people who believe the Internet can provide Christian community and that attendance in worship at a local church can be replaced by logging in. In an article entitled, "The Cyberchurch Is Coming," the Barna Research Group noted in one survey that 4 percent of the respondents said they use the Internet for religious or spiritual experiences. This number was relatively small, but the most important insight in the study was that "one out of six teens (16%) said that within the next five years they expect to use the Internet as a substitute for their current church-based religious experience."[2] Additionally, this comment was made mostly by teens who are currently regular church attendees.

A growing number of churches offer their worship experiences online. One of the more sophisticated is Bethel Tabernacle of Evansville, Indiana. Its Web site is called Zchurch. Two thousand people log in to Zchurch each week to join in the singing and prayers, and listen to the sermon. The difference between Zchurch and worship services that are broadcast on television is that Zchurch is interactive. Zchurch worshipers can offer prayers, chat about the sermon in real time, and later join an online Bible study or exchange email with other Zchurch participants.[3]

Is there any danger that "cyber *koinonia*" will replace the fellowship of a local church? Bruce B. Lawrence, chairman of the department of religion at Duke University, said, "The Net will dazzle and delight. But it will never replace what goes on inside the walls of a church."[4] Lawrence is correct, but the impact of the Internet on religious life will be greater than any of us can now predict. If it is true that a significant percentage of teens say they will find their primary religious and spiritual resources online, then we have yet to experience what the digital revolution will mean for the church.

One thing is certain, however. We dare not ignore the impact of the Internet on the life of the church. If we are to truly be responsible with the call God has given to us, we have an imperative to become literate in the field of new technologies.

Why Is This All So Threatening?

Why are so many of us intimidated by the computer, Internet, and digital revolution issue? Perhaps it's the strangeness of it all. The language is strange, the machines are strange, and even some of the people who are into this stuff are strange. Then there's the fact that we did not grow up with this technology. Radios, television, 16mm film projectors, cameras, and slide projectors were the things we learned to use. It was hard enough when the videocassette player came along. (Some of us still have those Beta format machines in our attics!) If we even learned to use the VCR, we usually still need our teens to program the thing. It's all so new and we've done just fine, thank you, up till now.

But there's more. The Internet can be a dangerous place for our children. True, there are always dangers when we are raising children, but this danger is more readily available to them because they often understand the technology and how to navigate within it better than do their parents. Those of us who can remember when our newly licensed teenage daughter or son took the car out for the first time have a handle on this Internet thing. When we handed over the keys to the car, and our teenager took off for the highway, we were at least more knowledgeable about cars than our children were. When we hand over the computer and agree to pay for online access, our children head out on a different kind of highway; a highway they have a lot more knowledge about than we do. That's scary stuff for a concerned parent.

If we could back up a generation or two, we would hear similar discussion about technologies that were new at the time, but are commonplace now. There were people who predicted the telephone would destroy authentic community because people would simply pick up the phone instead of talking with one another. Television, it was said, would interfere with family life and be harmful to our children's learning. Young people would watch more television and read fewer books. Some of the concerns were justified and the introduction of the term *couch potato* to our vocabulary is testimony to the fact that technology carries inherent risks. It is not these risks, however, that are the problem. It is lack of familiarity with the medium and the relationship of the person to the medium. We can relate to television as a helpful medium or we can allow it to dominate our lives and the lives of our children. It is our relationship with technological tools that makes the difference between technology as helpful servant and technology as harmful master. I will revisit this issue in chapter 5, "For Parents and Pastors."

How Technology Affects the Meaning of Ministry

The use of technology in the church's ministries provides amazing ways to enhance ministry. A church Web site can become a great way to keep communication in the church up to date. Email can keep people in touch. Computers can help liven up a Sunday school class and keep a youth group invested in the youth program. But, there is a danger we need to be aware of. It is absolutely essential that the local church pastor *not* become the lone technology resource for the church. In churches that are blessed with multiple staff, it is important that staff persons avoid becoming the only resource persons for technology.

During my seminary work, I took a course in the use of audio-visual equipment in the local church. While I actually ended up learning a lot about 16mm film projectors, overhead projectors, audiotape listening stations, and slide projectors, there were times when I wished I knew absolutely nothing about those devices. One of those times was when a woman in our church found me at a local restaurant and asked if I could come over to the church and change a lamp in the film projector. The youth group had rented a movie that was to be mailed back to the supplier the next morning, and she thought this was urgent enough to call me away from dinner.

The need for collaboration and teamwork is one of the advantages of the new technologies. No one person can do it all. Pastors can easily find themselves in the trap of doing it all, and there are lots of people and churches who are more than willing to let them do just that. Doing ministry as a lone ranger has never been theologically or ecclesiologically sound, but with the new possibilities available through new technologies, this approach is simply not possible. If, for instance, a church decides to enhance its prayer time during worship by using the Microsoft PowerPoint® presentation graphics program to create slides featuring members who are homebound or in nursing homes, advance planning and teamwork are essential.* While it would be *possible* for the pastor to take the photos, scan them into computer files, and hook up the LCD (liquid crystal display) projector to show the slides, it would not be *prudent* or good stewardship of the pastor's time and training to do so.[5]

The use of these new tools for enhancing our worship experience requires advance planning and production of materials. Solo ministry does not work in this new environment. The wonderful thing about the use of these new tools is the opportunity for collaboration and teamwork in planning for worship, education, youth work, and Internet-based ministry.

---

* Microsoft PowerPoint® is either a registered trademark or trademark of Microsoft Corporation in the United States and/or other countries.

New opportunities for ministry of the laity lie at the heart of computer-enhanced ministry (CEM). The idea of ministry of the laity is not a new thing at all. The apostle Paul wrote to the Roman church that "in one body we have many members, and not all the members have the same function." Indeed, "We have gifts that differ according to the grace given to us" (Romans 12:4, 6). When a church begins to use the new tools that have become available in the past few years, it will open doors for new people to participate in ministries of teaching, youth work, and worship.

During the early 1970s I served in a church as a youth and education pastor. We had the luxury of two worship services and two Sunday school hours. We decided to turn one of the Sunday school hours into an experimental learning opportunity for our children. This experiment was actually an early learning-center approach to education, or what some folks today are calling the "workshop rotation model" of Christian education. During one quarter, we decided to study our Congregational roots by building a Pilgrim church inside our fellowship hall. A few of the dads helped in constructing the actual building, pews, altar table, and all the furnishings. One of the fathers who was a carpenter served as the leader. Some of the moms sewed Pilgrim clothes and everyone joined in preparing the food. The concluding celebration for the last day of the quarter was a worship service. The dinner after worship was, of course, a highlight of the quarter.

It was amazing what we learned. Most of the people who helped in this quarter had never served as a Sunday school teacher, on the Board of Christian Education, or for that matter on *any* church committee. Our children's moms and dads knew more and shared more knowledge about Congregationalism in the Colonial period of United States history than we could ever have gained through an adult education course.

The implications for our generation are even greater. Many of the most sophisticated users of new technology are the young people in our congregations. One of the most exciting intergenerational possibilities for Christian education imaginable is having children and teenagers work with pastors and adult church leaders in creating new ways to communicate and teach the gospel. During our "Pilgrim church" experience, even our pastoral staff was amazed at the learning that took place, not only for the children, but most especially for the parents. So also, the invitation to our youngest members to use their gifts in the service of the church will result in Christian educational gains not seen in some time.

There is a critical principle here. When all of God's people—young, old, and in-between—use their gifts in service to the Body of Christ, the possibilities for the maturity of the church are multiplied exponentially.

New Wine Skins, Same Lord

Jesus' parable about the necessity of using new wineskins for new wine has some important things to say to the issue of using new technologies in ministry. The most familiar part of the parable is the warning against putting new wine into old wineskins. The result will be a complete loss of the new wine. New wineskins are required for new wine. Our purpose here, however, is to put the old wine into new wineskins. The less familiar line in the parable Jesus told is, "And no one after drinking old wine desires new wine, but says, 'The old is good' " (Luke 5:39). The good news of Jesus Christ is the fine wine with which we want to reach our world. It is clear that for our generation, the old wineskins are worn thin and new wineskins are needed if we are to preserve the good news and make it available to a new generation.

Maybe an example will help. If your church is like a lot of churches, you have lots of stuff tucked away in closets, attics, and storage rooms. (The basic principle is that the amount of stuff you have stored away in your church is directly proportional to the tendencies of the most prolific pack rat in your congregation.) One church I served lived in constant fear that one member would find out that someone threw out the gramophone her grandfather had given to the Sunday school. Do this exercise: Take a tour of your storage areas and count how many record players, View-Masters, film projectors, slide projectors, tape recorders, and other technological devices of the past are taking up space. This will make it clear that the church has always used technology.

It is not so much that there is resistance to using technology in the church as there is a resistance to using new or unfamiliar technology in the church. "Oliver Cromwell's Puritan movement, in power as of 1649, was responsible for destroying many organs in English [c]hurches. For the Puritans, the organ and its music represented anything but the piety and religiosity with which we often associate it."[6]

The issue is not organs, tape recorders, guitars, typewriters, or LCD projectors. The issue is the old wine that is good, the wine of the good news of Jesus Christ. The new technologies do not add anything to the good news, nor do they improve the old wine. This is one of the essential understandings of this book. The new wineskins that are available to us can make a world of difference in the communication of the good news to our generation. The apostle Paul wrote, "I have become all things to all people, that I might by all means save some. I do it all for the sake of the gospel, so that I may share in its blessings" (1 Corinthians 9:22*b*-23). It is safe to say that if Paul had to learn how to use an LCD projector or post a Web site to engage and evangelize the young people of his day, he would most likely consider the task a way to "by all means save some."

According to a study by the Pew Research Center, "17 million youth ages 12 and 17 use the Internet. That represents 73% of those in this age bracket."[7] The church is very much in need of persons who are literate in the new technologies. This need is particularly urgent when it comes to working with our children and young people.

Chapter Four

How the Landscape Has Changed

The Impact of Technology on Our Culture

One of the most significant ways to come to grips with how dramatically technology has changed our culture is to recognize the way we view time. For many of us, golden oldies on the radio go back to the days when Bing Crosby, Frank Sinatra, and Guy Lombardo were big in the music industry. For others of us there is a shock when a song is referred to as a golden oldie and we suddenly realize twenty years have gone by very quickly.

Change in technology occurs at a stunning rate. It is not uncommon for technology reporters on television and technology writers in our newspapers and magazines to use language like "way back in 1997." It is only since 1997 that the American Registry for Internet Numbers was established.[1] In January 1995 there were 4,852,000 computers with Internet addresses (Web sites). As of July 1997 the number was 19,540,000. By July 2000 the best guess was that there were 93,047,785 Internet addresses on the World Wide Web.[2] Estimates about how many people will be online in the future are only guesstimates. No one can say for sure. We can be sure, however, that the absolute majority of our church members will have Internet access and nearly 100 percent of their children will have online access in school if not at home.

The growth of television use in American households provides a picture of how the Internet will likely become mainstream for all of us. In 1950, television was relatively new and expensive. Only 9 percent of households in the United States had television sets. In the relatively short time span from 1950 to 1955, the number of households with television sets was up to 64.5 percent. By 1999 the figure was 98.2 percent.[3]

Remember the neighborhood television and household appliance repairman? Most have gone the way of drive-in movie theaters. When a television set goes on the fritz today, we put it out with the garbage and purchase a new model. Your grandmother would be absolutely stunned to hear that a television set is now disposable.

The personal computer was a luxury for most households just ten years ago. The drop in prices for the personal computer, along with much more user-friendly software, has made the personal computer a mainstream household item. Annual surveys of Internet access have been conducted by the National Center for Education Statistics. In the fall of 1994, 35 percent of public schools had access to the Internet. The fall 2000 survey showed that 98 percent of all public schools in the United States had Internet access.[4]

Television has played a significant role in our culture and has had an impact on entertainment, education, the economy, and even health. Yet, the Internet and personal computer revolution hold even more potential for our culture. No segment of life as we know it has been left untouched. Marianne McGee in the online magazine *Information Week* noted that economists once doubted whether technology would have much effect on productivity in the United States. However, McGee wrote, "last month [March 2000], Federal Reserve economists released a study showing the use of IT [information technology] and the production of IT products has contributed approximately $50 billion in productivity output annually since the mid-1990s. That $50 billion figure represents about two-thirds of an annual $70 billion productivity gain overall demonstrated by U.S. businesses in the last half of the 1990s."[5]

Information technology has profoundly changed the way teaching and learning take place. Growing numbers of teacher education programs require courses in educational technology. The U.S. Department of Education maintains an Office of Educational

Technology, which has among its priorities that "all students and teachers will have universal access to effective information technology in their classrooms, schools, communities, and homes."[6]

The state of Iowa had a vision for technology use in education in the late 1980s and early 1990s. Iowa developed the most extensive fiber-optic system in the country. Fiber-optic cable was buried in Iowa's ninety-nine counties by November 1993. The network was built so that every citizen in Iowa, especially those in rural areas, would have access to educational resources. Today, education, medicine, the court system, and government all make extensive use of the system. Every citizen of Iowa lives within fifteen miles of an Iowa Communications Network (ICN) video classroom. The educational experience of thousands of young people has been enhanced in a way that most of us would never have imagined in our school years. One example of the impact of ICN technology on the learning experience of schoolchildren is found in a trip across Africa. Iowa children and young people were able to share in the journey with those who actually made the trip.

Through the use of ICN video, students in classrooms throughout the state were able to explore right along with a team of adventurers as they traveled across Africa by bicycle and a few months later retraced Charles Darwin's 1835 journey to the Galapagos Islands.

Through these full-motion, two-way, interactive experiences, elementary, middle, and high school students got a taste of the culture, geography, and wildlife in other corners of the world. In addition to the video component of the programs, students were able to follow the team's adventures via the Internet and give input on where the team should travel next and what they should study along the way.[7]

The technology to deliver these experiences to our home desktop computers is available now and will become commonplace in the next two or three years. Perhaps you have seen the television commercial where an elementary school-age child is in bed, pretending to be ill and too sick to go to school. The child's mother goes to the computer and says, "That's okay, honey, we can download your homework!" It does not take a lot of imagination to figure that we could also get the children's Sunday school lessons, a Sunday sermon, or the adult study material from the Internet when we cannot be in church on Sunday morning.

The impact of new technologies on our culture is one of those major events in human history that rank with the invention of the printing press and the industrial revolution. Just as Johannes Gutenberg, Alexander Graham Bell, or Henry Ford could never have imagined where their work would take the world, so even the most imaginative of us do not have a clue as to the eventual impact of the new technologies on our lives. Mark this down. *All* of us will feel the impact. Some of us may welcome the change while others dread or even despise it, but the fact is, *all* of us will be affected by it.

A personal example will illustrate. My wife let me know in no uncertain terms some years ago that she wanted little or nothing to do with my fondness of or expenditures for technology. She grudgingly went along with my loan application seeking four thousand dollars for a computer and printer. The printer alone cost $1,500 and weighed at least forty pounds. I could not interest her in the arcane appearance of the black and white computer screen with all its strange language. She did not share my delight in the ability to manage our checkbook and write articles on this machine.

"You do your computing," she said, "and I will do my garage sales."

And there's the rub. I despise garage sales—not the ones you go to, but the ones you hold at your own residence. If God granted the prayers of this poor servant, I would never have to be a part of managing a garage sale at my home. I consider myself a major contributor to the concept of "for better or for worse, in sickness and in health" because I have from time to time endured what was for me the agony of helping with a weekend garage sale. "If only there was another way," I habitually moaned.

And God is gracious! As the years went by and the Internet became a part of our lives, I discovered "The Antiques Roadshow" Web site.

"Honey," I said one day, "come here. You have to see this."

She resisted. I had from time to time attempted to interest her in one thing or another on the Internet and to date it had been a bust.

But this was the day God smiled on me. She actually joined me at the computer.

"What's that?" she exclaimed.

"It's the 'Antiques Roadshow' Web site," I answered.

With this small introduction, she is now a regular user of the computer. In fact, we now have two computers and she is one of eBay's most avid salespersons. It is the best of both worlds. She has her virtual garage sales, and I no longer have the next on-site garage sale hanging over my head. A bonus is that since she managed to talk her three sisters into getting Internet access and email, our phone bills have decreased considerably. I should point out, however, that our shopping bills have inched up as she has joined me in the exploding world of e-commerce.

New technologies have changed the world as we know it. Education, the economy, communication, and vocation have all changed dramatically as the personal computer moved from luxury item to familiar article to necessity for most homes.

A TV Generation in an Internet-Generation World

Many of us in the church qualify as the TV generation. Some of us grew up with Ozzie and Harriet, Howdy Doody, and *American Bandstand*. Those of us who are leaders in the church today are the children and grandchildren of those Tom Brokaw described in his book *The Greatest Generation*. Our media world was dominated by Hollywood movies and New York television. Television grew in influence and economic significance as the drive-in theater went the way of the dinosaur. Some of us baby boomers can remember those evenings when our parents would whisk us—children still in our pajamas carrying blankets and pillows—to the local drive-in theater to see a movie in the privacy of the family car. After intermission and a stomach full of popcorn and soda, we drifted off to sleep in the backseat of the car while Mom and Dad watched the conclusion of a feature film.

One enduring figure of the late 1950s still binds generations together. Dick Clark with his *American Bandstand* remained on our cultural stage during the 1950s, 1960s, 1970s, and 1980s. Many of us can still recall the songs that vied for top spot on the show as we watched in anticipation while young people cast their votes for the best song of the show. The careers of countless musical artists were launched by Dick Clark on *American Bandstand*.

One of the primary ways to understand just how much technology has changed our world is in the entertainment industry. Our young folk no longer sit back and watch as their contemporaries on television pick the songs and the stars. They actually join in the voting and participate in the outcome of what is taking place on television. Host Carson Daly draws hundreds of thousands of young people to a show called *TRL*, or *Total Request Live*. Each day *TRL* plays the music videos of those artists who received the most votes from young people who go online to vote for their favorite song. An adult version of this entertainment is offered by networks. A court case is done in the style of a newsmagazine and the audience is invited to get online and cast their votes of "not guilty" or "guilty" along with other opinions about the case. The results are compared with the jury verdict at the end of the show.

This is a change in the way things work for many of us. Learning, entertainment, economics, and communication have a participatory quality. *Interactive* is one of the new buzzwords. Entertainment is no longer simply passively watching, it is actively joining in. Learning is not passive, but collaborative. Investing does not need to be a mysterious enterprise conducted by remote persons on Wall Street, but a part of our personal banking activities. Taking care of the family banking no longer has to be conducted Monday through Friday from 9 to 5, but can be done online after the evening news or on a Saturday afternoon.

One of the reasons many of us find the new technologies so difficult is that it is no easy thing being a TV-generation person in an Internet-generation world. However, lest we find ourselves falling into stereotypical thinking, I should tell you about the lunchtime conversation I had with an eighty-three-year-old woman at a denominational gathering. She was concerned about her computer's abilities since her great-grandson was going to be spending more time at her home. "Can you tell me," she asked, "whether I should go ahead with cable access, or is there some way I can tweak my system to allow for better downloads of the MP3 files my great-grandson likes to listen to? I do have a Pentium III processor, but I suspect we'll have a bandwidth problem if I don't go with cable. I'm pretty sure we do not have DSL available in our town." In plain English she was asking if the music her great-grandson wanted to listen to on her computer's sound system would take too long to download from the Internet. Music files tend to be very large and can take a long time to get from a server to a local computer by means of the Internet. Most young folks won't wait ten minutes for a song to become available over the Internet.

To be sure, this is a remarkable great-grandmother, but with a bit of motivation all of us can learn the basics of computer-enhanced ministry and discover the potential of the new technological tools.

The Impact of Technology on Teaching, Learning, and Worshiping in the Church

The impact of technology for our ministry in the church can hardly be overstated. There is a gap between the opportunities available to the ministry of the church through use of the new technologies and the actual readiness of the church to use them. That's a key reason for this book. One of the ways we at the University of Dubuque Theological Seminary are working to overcome this gap is through introducing technology courses to the seminary curriculum. One student who is training to become a local church pastor turned in a report on an assignment in which students had to apply new technologies in the ministry of Christian education. The assignment she chose was to visit three Internet sites. One focused on sermon preparation, one on Sunday school material, and one on local-church Internet ministry. Her response was typical of many who first discover the wealth of material that is available on the Internet. "What a wonderful assignment! This was amazing. I consider myself fairly proficient in using the computer and email, and I do use the

Internet, but I had no idea how much was available. I discovered Sunday school and preaching resources that will become absolutely invaluable to my ministry."

Just as technology has changed our culture, so it also will have an effect on the teaching, learning, and worshiping life of the church. This does not, repeat, *does not* mean, "out with the old and in with the new," as though the central content of worship and teaching will change. It *does* mean that there will be wonderful ways to enhance and make more available our ministry to the people of our local church.

Some years ago, the VCR made it possible for local churches to take their worship services to members of the church who were homebound or in nursing homes. If you have ever had the opportunity to bring a tape of your worship service to a dedicated homebound member of your church, you have seen the power of technology do something wonderful. Imagine what it would be like for the congregation to see an image of this homebound member during prayer time at Sunday morning worship as they prayed for all shut-in members of the church. What if your youth group were to offer three or four interviews with these oldest members of the church as a part of your time of sharing in the service? Imagine what this kind of interchange could mean for worship and the building up of the family of faith. Would it surprise you to know that for less than $300, a youth group could make video recordings of your oldest members talking about their experience in the church and then put all of these videos on a CD for others to see? Not only that, but this $300 would allow you to produce future CDs for $1.50 each.

Here's another scenario. Imagine a confirmation service. On the screen at the front of the sanctuary there is a video recording of a child in first grade singing "Jesus Loves Me." The video is playing while a ninth grader is kneeling to receive prayers of confirmation. The child singing in the video is the ninth grader who is being confirmed. No one in the congregation has a dry eye, and the awesome responsibility of raising our children in faith is driven home like never before.

Finally, a family who tries faithfully to have their children present each Sunday morning for Sunday school is pressured by the need to care for aging parents in another town. They simply are not able to keep what they would like to be an every-Sunday commitment to attend Sunday school. Another family in the church is a blended family. Two out of four children spend every other weekend with a father and a stepmother who do not attend church. Fortunately, the Christian education department of the church has decided to make weekly resources available to families through the church's Web site.

Not only do these families have more options and resources available to them, the material is available in a format that invites the interest of the children. All of these things are possible for most local churches, and we will visit some of these technologies in succeeding chapters. The University of Dubuque Theological Seminary has developed a certificate program in "Ministry and Technology" to respond to the need for training in the use of new technologies in the church. A Web site for this program may be found at *http://udts.dbq.edu/CMT.htm.*

The essential thing to understand is that anyone can learn to use the technologies that have emerged in the past few years. It is not so difficult as many have imagined. We have used technology for decades. Whether it was a slide projector, a 16mm film projector, a camera, or even a radio, we learned how to use tools that made it possible to liven up our Sunday school classes and study groups.

To be sure, there were terrible films, distasteful radio programs, and horrible television programs we did not want our children to watch, but we would likely not do away with film, radio, or television. We have learned to use the good and avoid the bad. The issues are the same even though the technologies are different. With a bit of courage and a desire to reach the next generation of disciples, we can give our children and young people the leadership they deserve. We can make the ministry of our church available to many who have been left out.

The impact of new technologies on the life of the church may represent the most exciting opportunity for evangelism and discipleship that has come to us in generations. We dare not miss it.

Chapter Five

For Parents and Pastors

Special Concerns for Parents

IS THE INTERNET SAFE?

The Internet provides a whole new way for intruders to get into our homes. Parents in Madison, Wisconsin, had a close encounter with tragedy when an intruder entered their home and took their fifteen-year-old daughter captive.

This intruder, however, never set foot in the family home. He came through an online chat room. The mom and dad were oblivious to a relationship their daughter had formed with a fifty-five-year-old man. Fortunately, this story had a happier ending than many. Police located the pair just before they crossed the Mexican border.

If your home has Internet access, this means you can get "out there" and surf the Web. However, the access goes both ways, and people like this cyberpedophile are able to get "in there." Children and teenagers are going online by the thousands every day. A survey in late 2000 by the Pew Internet and American Life project showed that 73 percent of young people between the ages of twelve and seventeen go online.[1] This also means increased access for intruders who seek entry into our homes.

What's a parent to do? Some have vowed to simply unplug the computer and cancel the online account. However, this eliminates educational resources that can give our children a tremendous advantage in their educational journeys. In spite of the pitfalls, the potential of new technologies for our education both in school and at church is just beginning to take shape. Collaborative confirmation classes for small churches, local church outreach, and quality resources for family living are all available through new and emerging technologies. The answer to the technological challenge facing the church today is not to bury our heads in the sand and wish the whole Internet had never happened, but instead to equip pastors and families to use these powerful new tools.

How to Supervise Your Children's Use of the Internet

Supervising children's activities is no new thing for most parents reading this book. It is natural for concerned parents to watch over their children, and this is even more critical when it comes to leisure time. Many children in our culture spend countless hours sitting in front of television sets or standing in front of video games down at the arcade, and almost no one is checking on what they are watching or playing. It should not surprise us that these children are more likely to have difficulty in school, poor social skills, and poor health.[2]

A few years ago, a Sunday school teacher came to ask if I would speak to the parents of a boy in her first-grade class. This young lad had used language and told stories in front of the other children that could only have come from an X-rated movie. When the teacher asked him where he had heard and seen such things, he replied, "On television." It turned out that the boy's parents had left the boy and his older brother home alone with access to the pay-per-view channels of their cable television service. Though the parents were horrified and embarrassed that this had happened, they soon realized they could have prevented this from happening by taking the simple step of putting a block on their pay-per-view service.

The block was instituted quickly for this particular family, but the fact remains that we live in a culture where countless numbers of children live in environments where no one is watching. When a computer with access to the Internet is added to a home where no one is watching, the result can be harmful and even dangerous.

Potential hazards involved in Internet usage are readily apparent. One quick trip through these examples should alert any parent to the fact that supervision in all our children's activities is essential, but supervision in our children's online activity is critical.

- There are an estimated one hundred thousand Web sites involved . . . in child pornography.[3]
- From January 2000 to March 2001, the U.S. Customs Cyber Smuggling Center in Fairfax, Virginia, reviewed more than ten thousand tips.[4]
- Internet gambling has become a billion-dollar industry. Although there has been strong effort to pass a ban on Internet gambling, the chances of passage are rated as slim. Even government officials concede that banning Internet gambling will be unlikely to happen anytime soon.

  Arizona Senator Jon Kyl had some interesting things to say about the [Internet Gambling Prohibition Act].

  When asked about the Bill's prospects for 2001, Kyl said: "I think that would be very difficult. The amount of money in Internet gambling is so great now that it has become a multi-billion-dollar industry."

  Even Senator Richard Bryan, one of the Bill's biggest supporters, agreed with Kyl, saying the measure's prospects look bleak. "I believe next year Internet gambling will have reached critical mass, and there is very little likelihood to get prohibition."[5]

- Gambling and porn sites are two examples of the fact that Internet activity can become addictive. A study by Dr. Keith J. Anderson of the Rensselaer Polytechnic Institute noted that "approximately 10 percent of Internet-using students have used the Internet to the degree that their usage meets criteria that are parallel to those of other forms of dependence."[6] Addictive use of the Internet has affected men, women, children, the workplace, and our homes.[7]

- Pedophiles online or "cyberpredators" are lurking in chat rooms and have built thousands of Web sites where they prey upon children.

Excursus

A brief personal note to parents: By now, many parents may be thinking, *Forget it! Who needs the Internet?* I promise you, as involved as I am in information technology and the World Wide Web, I recoil when I hear and read stories of the bad things that can happen with Internet access. It would be tempting to say, "Who needs this extra problem? No Internet for this family!" I have a six-year-old daughter who does not need another force in her life that will test her vulnerabilities. It is difficult enough to teach her about "danger stranger" without having to worry about "danger stranger" right in our own home.

Nevertheless, I do not want to make a decision that will cut her off from the absolutely amazing world of information and education that is available to her through the Internet. I can provide her with access to more information, education, and research material for less money than my parents would have paid for a second-rate set of encyclopedias when I was her age. There is no question that providing her with access to the Internet will mean a little more work and a little more devotion to family. The bottom line, however, is that I want her to have the same access to the advantages of a whole new world of information that the majority of her peers have.

The reality is that she will have access to the Internet. If she cannot access the Internet at home, she will do so at school, the public library, or at most of her friends' homes.

The issue for our family then is not *whether* we will be involved with the Internet at home, but *how* we will be involved. Think of it this way. Driving can be a dangerous activity for teenagers. The University of Michigan's Health System noted in an article on its Web site that "each year, more than 10,000 people ages 16 to 25 die as the result of alcohol use and half of these deaths result from crashes caused by alcohol impaired driving."[8] There is one way I can be sure that my daughter will not become one of these statistics. I could deny her the opportunity to learn to drive and make sure she does not have access to the family automobile. For that matter, I could guarantee that she would never become one of the missing children statistics by locking her in a closet until she reaches age twenty-one.

If you happen to be one of those parents who simply are not ready to deal with the still mystical world of computers and the information superhighway, sit down, take a deep breath, and think about it.

Your children *will* drive a car.

Your children *will* venture out of the house.

Your children *will* become a part of the online generation.

The only question is, Under what circumstances will they become a part of this new generation using new tools? I want to let you in on how we will address the issue of using the Internet in our family. The basic principles should translate into your family as well. The fact that you are reading this text is evidence that you care very much about the spiritual and moral development of the children in your family and in your church. Whether it is television, movies, or surfing the Internet, it is our values that determine what is seen, heard, or "surfed" in our homes. There are three commitments we as parents need to make when we link our home to the information superhighway.

1. Make some advance decisions about the way you will use the computer in your home. Thinking through some ground rules ahead of time will help smooth the transition to becoming a family with Internet access.

2. Talk with your children about specific ways that you as a family *will* and *will not* use the Internet. If you are in the process of buying a computer, you are in a great position to approach the purchase with an agreement for computer and Internet use in place. If you already have a computer, but do not have Internet access, you can build a similar agreement before opening the information superhighway. If you are already living with a bit of Internet chaos, you will have to lay down the law, call a family conference, and gently impose some guidelines and rules.

3. Commit to gaining specific knowledge about safe use of the Internet.[9]

Family-Friendly Internet and Safe Surfing

Here are a few questions to help parents think through how they will approach computer and Internet use as a family:

- *Where will the computer be located?* Many families place the computer in a location used by the whole family instead of placing it in a child's room. This reinforces the idea that computer use will be a family activity. Making this decision to at least begin the use of the computer and the Internet as a family activity will set the foundation for the values and goals that will guide future use.
- *How much time will be spent using the computer and accessing the Internet?* This depends upon what use the computer will have. Will it be used primarily for entertainment or education? Will the family finances be kept on the computer or will the computer be primarily for children's use? Most families discover that increased familiarity with the computer's potential brings increased use. An eventual struggle for time on the computer inevitably comes with the territory.
- *What priorities will govern our computer use?* There are so many ways a computer can be used that it is essential to have some guidelines in place about who gets to use it, for how long, and at what time. You might decide that homework comes before entertainment. So Billy's need to do some research for a school paper comes before Sally's "need" to chat with her friends. As demand for use grows, you will soon find your arbitration skills in demand. If you have more than one child, mournful cries of "I need the computer" will grow exponentially within a week. You will be amazed at how true this is even if none of your children had a clue about computers the day you took it out of the box and began to hook it up.
- *How will we integrate all these new activities into our family?*

The key to developing a family-friendly use of the Internet is to decide that you will learn together. The available activities range from surfing the Net to using email, participating in newsgroups, and joining in chat rooms. You can plan on the fact that by the time you have a handle on surfing the Net, your children will be using all the tools available. Learn together and invite them to teach you as they learn.

- *Take one step at a time with your family.* Visit some Internet sites together that relate to schoolwork or various family members' hobbies. Next, you might set up one email account and see how it goes by writing to family and friends who are online. Some ISPs allow several email accounts, and each family member can set up a personal account if you wish. If you decide to use chat rooms, visit one or two recommended chat rooms with your children to get a sense for how they work.

Several organizations and Web sites publish guidelines for children and teens who use the Internet.[10] The following "Ten Commandments of Safe Surfing" deal with the issues most commonly addressed in these guidelines. These commandments are intended for elementary school–age children. They can be adapted for your teens.

1. You shall honor your parents and tell them about any bad language you see online.
2. You shall tell your parents about any stranger who sends an email to you.
3. You shall not agree to meet with any stranger who sends an email to you. You shall tell your parents or your teacher about strangers who invite any family member or friend to meet with them.
4. You shall not give your name, address, or phone number to any stranger who asks for it.
5. You shall not give the name of your school to any stranger who asks for it.
6. You shall not give any password you use to anyone except a parent. You shall not give your password even to your best friend.

7. You shall not give personal information about yourself or your family to anyone in a chat room.

8. You shall not click on any Internet address (URL) sent to you in emails from strangers, and you shall notify your parents or teachers about any emails you receive that contain URLs.

9. You shall tell your parents or teachers immediately about any bad pictures or bad words you see on your computer screen.

10. When you use the computer, you shall remember to love the Lord your God with all your heart and all your soul and all your mind.

Many families soon discover that time on the computer is a precious commodity. One family checkbook, two high schoolers with homework assignments, one elementary schoolchild who loves the Sesame Street Web site, and one parent who pursues a hobby online will soon stress the available time on the family computer.

It will not be long before you hear the words "I need my own computer." One of the best ways to handle the time crunch with a family computer is to provide a second computer for homework assignments, term papers, and other basic tasks. If you find yourself in this predicament, the second computer can be relatively inexpensive. A second computer could serve the need for additional computer time in a growing family and would not need to have Internet access. Keep the Internet access with the family computer.

As time goes on, all family members will become more familiar with the computer and Internet use. This will make decisions about family computing needs easier.

Family computer use can be compared to the changes we have encountered with the telephone. Many of us remember when one telephone was all a family needed. The family telephone served some very basic needs, and extension telephones were a luxury. Sometime in the 1950s, the telephone became a major communication vehicle for teenagers. An extension phone in the teen's room became standard, and it was not long before many families had a second phone line for the children. This system is archaic for today's teens. Children today consider themselves deprived if their parents refuse to get them a cell phone. Each family will respond to its telephone needs based on its particular circumstances, finances, and ability to distinguish between needs and wants. So also, every family will have its own approach to the issue of how to configure a computing solution.

Positive Uses of the Internet for Building the Family

In spite of the fact that there is much negative content on the Web, there are wonderful ways to build communication and learn together on the Internet. Here is a sampling of ideas you will find on my companion Web site, *www.newtools-online.com:*

- Family devotions have fallen on hard times in our hectic society, but here's a way to have fun together at the computer and at the same time learn more about the Bible. There is an Internet site called Bible Tutor (*www.bibletutor.luthersem.edu*) that provides a basic Bible knowledge program complete with quizzes. The site has a basic level that is free and an advanced level that can be purchased.[11] There are Bible knowledge quizzes that can be taken online, and these would make great family activity or devotion times.
- A great learning resource is available at the Encyclopaedia Britannica's Web site (*www.britannica.com*). One of the many things you can do is to make a world tour of countries you would like to visit as a family. There are extensive articles and information available on the countries of the world. Doing something together at the Britannica site will give your children good exposure to an Internet resource that will help when they begin to use the computer for their homework.
- Younger children will enjoy the U.S. Department of Education's site, PBS Kids (*www.pbskids.org*). There are sites and activities for all of the younger children's favorite television shows. Aimed at younger children, this site will help build the computing skills of children in their K–3 years.

• Christian resources can provide information, activities, and guidance for family issues. You will discover quickly that the difficulty with the Internet is simply sorting through the mountains of available material. I recommend beginning with the following three sites, which will provide a broad range of good resources to begin your online activity. Links to the sites are listed on the companion Web site (*www.newtools-online.com*). The magazine, *Christianity Today,* sponsors the first site: *www.gospelcom.net* has extensive online Christian resources including online Bible versions and devotions. The site *www.forministry.com* is sponsored by the American Bible Society and has resources for parents, families, pastors, and churches. Another site, *www.beliefnet.com,* is a broad-based religious resource that includes information on the major world religions. These sites and more will be found on the companion Web site.

The main advantage of making computer usage and Internet access a family activity is that by doing so, you ensure a level of accountability and discipline. This new technology has a lot of potential—potential for good and potential for evil. When we as parents are involved in computing with our children, we tip the balance in favor of the potential being good.

On April 20, 1999, Eric Harris and Dylan Klebold killed twelve classmates and one teacher at Columbine High School in Littleton, Colorado. It was not long after the shooting that the issue of computer games and violent Internet content was brought up. The *Rocky Mountain News* on May 2, 1999, carried a story in which reporters Mike Anton and Lisa Ryckman wrote of the boys, "They were die-hard gamers who loved the interactive bloodbath called DOOM, which arms players to the teeth and pits them against legions of homicidal demons lurking in an endless maze.

"Harris always had top-of-the-line equipment, even when they first met as freshmen four years ago. Together, they gamed, they hacked, they created and modified programs. They found power through technology."[12] Eric Harris had created a Web site where he expressed the hatred and violence that filled his troubled mind.

Game Deputy is a software that can analyze games on a computer and report on the level of violence, as well as point parents to reviews of computer games and thus enable some parental control over the use of computer games. Game Deputy has an interview on the company Web site with game author Ernest Adams. The subject of the article is the relationship between computer games and violence. Adams is no fan of banning or antiviolence legislation regarding computer games, yet he offers these comments: "I believe it's up to the parents to decide whether their family is going to entertain itself together or separately. In my own family, my brother and I were not allowed to choose how we entertained ourselves all the time. Some of the time we entertained ourselves separately, but at other times our parents decided that the family would do something together.

"I'd say that it's really important to play games with your children, including computer games, even if it seems boring to you as an adult. The only way a kid learns to be a good loser or a gracious winner is by example—backed up by enforced standards of behavior. You can't be sure they're getting that example from other kids. Watch what kinds of games they're playing, and make sure they're appropriate.

"And, as my parents did, take control of the entertainment agenda. Children nowadays often spend as much time with the TV or the computer as they do at school. Obviously children need some freedom to control their own leisure time, but that control shouldn't be unlimited."[13]

Mark this down: The top three principles in a parent's arsenal of Internet safety strategies are: information, supervision, and participation.

The Pastor and the Internet

THE PASTOR'S LEADERSHIP ROLE IN TECHNOLOGY

The average seminary student at the University of Dubuque Theological Seminary is forty-four years old, and the student population is evenly divided according to gender. Some students are in their fifties and even sixties, and some are in their late twenties and early thirties. Many have families, and a significant number serve churches as student pastors. Student demographics in most mainline seminaries are similar. The old stereotypes are gone. There are no age, gender, or marital status barriers, and young students (meaning right out of college) are in the minority. But there is one significant issue that divides the students. One group of students come to class with notebooks and pens and take lecture notes the way most of us once did. These students write as fast as they can. The second group of students come to class with portable computers, and each person takes lecture notes as fast as he or she can. Then they frequently send the lecture notes as an email attachment to a friend or friends who were not able to attend class.

Many students in this latter group have taken a short course in using the computer and Internet for biblical and theological research. All students will have a section devoted to educational technology in their basic Christian education course. They anticipate supplying leadership in technology use in the churches they will serve.

Clergy are not different from the general population when it comes to technology use. The Pew Research Center published a study that addressed the issue of who is planning to go online and who has no plans to use the Internet. Among the findings of the study were these observations:

> Most of the strongest Internet holdouts are older Americans, who are fretful about the online world and often don't believe it can bring them any benefits. In contrast, a substantial majority of those under 30 who are not currently online say they plan to get access, though the expense of going online still looms as a major issue to them. This suggests that over an extended period of time, perhaps in a generation, Internet penetration will reach the levels enjoyed by the telephone, which is used by 94% of Americans, and the television, which is used by 98% of Americans. Among those most likely to say they plan to get Internet access are parents with children living at home.[14]

This latter statistic is of most significance for pastors. The generation that is already in our Sunday schools is the generation that will make computer and Internet use as common as telephone use. One of the statistics in the Pew study was that "63% of parents with children under 18 who don't now have Internet access say they will probably or definitely go online"[15]

If there is no other reason for pastors to become computer and Internet literate, this alone should suffice. Our church's young families and children are going to be very much involved with the new technologies. If we are to use every means possible to reach out to and be in communication with our young folk, we would no more turn away from the Internet than we would get rid of our telephones. This is not to deny that it is sometimes a marvelous thing to turn off the telephone, the television, and the computer! A great personal goal for clergy is to have a weekly fast from all of these gadgets.

When we use the Internet as a source for church-related work, we will encounter one of the realities of the online world. The number one factor that drives the Internet is economics. This results in a lot of advertising in an Internet world that is heavily slanted toward e-commerce. Searching for scholarly resources will take a bit more effort than searching for a stockbroker. However, the fact remains that one of the great benefits for pastors going online is the availability of research and study materials for local church ministry. Denominational and educational institutions, along with many private individuals, have posted material on the Internet that makes important resources available while saving both time and money.

One of the most significant studies that have been produced to date on the impact of technology for the church is a Pew Research Center report on the use of the Internet in American churches and synagogues. More than thirteen hundred congregations participated in the study. The study contains a wealth of information on how the Internet has been used in congregations and what the prospects are for continued growth of Internet use. The complete study is available online.[16] The report would be an excellent resource for pastors to use with a group of persons from the local church who have an interest in working to help the church get up to speed with Internet technology.

Study and Sermon Preparation Resources for Pastors

A significant motivational factor in clergy use of the Internet is the wealth of resources available for study, sermon preparation, and worship services. My work with sermonhelp.com began in 1997 and is entering its fourth year and its second journey through the lectionary cycle. Since the beginning, the number of inquiries from local church pastors, interim ministers, and lay speakers has increased fourfold. I would estimate that 50 percent of these inquiries are from persons who indicate they are new to the Internet and frequently ask for some assistance in using their computers and navigating the Internet.

Feedback from pastors about this service reflects the variety of ways sermon material on the Internet can help in the demanding work of parish ministry.

"I find this resource invaluable during those hectic weeks all of us have. I run out of time before I run out of demands on my time, and I am grateful for help on those infrequent Saturday nights when there has simply not been time to craft a complete sermon."

"The thing I find most helpful about this service is that it jump-starts my own thinking about the text."

"I don't actually use the sermons as they are written, but they have become my devotional reading. As a preaching minister, I miss out on hearing a sermon. This has helped me to 'hear' others preach."

"I check in on sermonhelp.com only occasionally. I guess it has become my 'pinch hitter'!"

Internet-based resources for preaching ministry can be divided into the two basic areas of study resources and sermon and worship preparation resources. The most extensive site for study of the weekly lectionary texts I know of is the site *www.textweek.com,* which is authored and maintained by Jenee Woodard. As well as featuring resources for the weekly lectionary texts, the site contains a movie and art concordance that relates the weekly text to themes in film and art. It is possible to begin at textweek.com and from there find a world of resources including specific sermon preparation sites. Some of the sites are free and some are available by subscription. One advantage of a subscription service like sermonhelp.com is the ability to have consistent resources available several weeks in advance.

In the past three years, sermon resource sites have grown exponentially, and it is easy to get lost and spend inordinate amounts of time sorting through them. The companion Web site to this volume will have links to a few of the best sites currently available. In addition, there is a significant list of links to valuable study and research resources. One pastor who received this list of links wrote, "This is like having a whole wall of books I could never afford!"

Internet-Based Opportunities for Parish Ministry

Most congregations that use technological tools in ministry have found email use very helpful. Email is more widely used than any other tool and its use predates the Internet explosion.

One example of pastoral use of email illustrates how effective this tool can be. Dr. Kenneth R. Bickel, senior pastor of the First Congregational United Church of Christ, in Dubuque, Iowa, has an email list that he uses once or twice every week. When you meet Dr. Bickel or visit the church, he will inevitably ask, "Do you have an email address?" If you do, he will write the address down and ask if he can put you in his email newsletter group.

Before the week is up, you will receive Ken's email newsletter called *Church Matters*. This email project takes a time commitment, but Pastor Bickel believes his increased contact with church members is worth the time.

Email can be used in a number of ways in the church. Groups can be set up for committees, Bible study groups, and Sunday school, among others. Chapter 13 will list a number of other ideas that can be implemented in most local churches that have a computer and Internet access.

A Note to Local Church Leaders and Teachers

I have discussed the cultural and technological reasons why the use of new technologies is important for the church. Members of today's churches, especially our younger members and a growing number of families, are finding more ways to use the computer and Internet. The number of pastors online is on the rise as they discover the benefits. With families and pastors using the Internet more frequently, there is one final ingredient that can bring about effective use of new technological tools in ministry. That ingredient is having a leadership in the local church that is committed to helping the church integrate ministry and technology. Without an involved leadership, the impact of new technologies in the church tends to grow in a haphazard way. Support from local church leadership and good planning will produce a clear vision of how the church can take advantage of ministry-enhancing tools. Appoint a task force or group to work with the pastor in developing a plan. The Pew Research Center report mentioned earlier is a good resource to help with this effort.

The most promising place for a quick start in using technology for ministry is in the area of youth and Christian education. The clientele are by and large already familiar with the tools and can likely help teach their teachers and leaders how to use them. In many churches, youth work and education are in need of a boost, and this could be one of the more receptive and rewarding areas of ministry in which to apply new tools and new methods.[17]

Part Three

NEW TOOLS
FOR MINISTRY

T his section offers an introduction to using technological tools
to enhance the ministry of the local church. A short tutorial
on Microsoft PowerPoint and Microsoft FrontPage Express®
will start your learning curve.* The ministry focus is in the three
areas of education and youth ministry, Internet-based ministry (your
Web presence), and media arts in worship.

---

* Microsoft FrontPage Express® is either a registered trademark or trademark
of Microsoft Corporation in the United States and/or other countries.

Chapter Six

Audiovisuals with a New Twist

From Filmstrip to Laptop:
An Introduction to Equipment

Most of you remember well the filmstrips that once supplemented the Sunday school curriculum. Indeed, it is likely that many of our churches still have at least one shoebox full of filmstrips that have not been out of their 35mm containers for years. But in its day, the filmstrip was a wonderful tool. Accompanying audiocassette tapes made the lesson exciting, and children were engrossed in the sights and sounds of biblical stories.

The last Sunday school teacher I know of who used a filmstrip and audiotape about the life of the apostle Paul in her class was dismayed by the reaction of her fifth-grade class. "They laughed," she exclaimed. "They actually thought I showed it as a joke!"

Filmstrip technology was great in its day. It captured the attention of children and adults for a period of time. Filmstrips were the ideal example of the adage "a picture is worth a thousand words," and filmstrip pictures along with an audiotape beat a teacher or committee chairperson's presentation hands down. There are some educators in both public and church-school education who still see a place for filmstrips in the curriculum; nevertheless, the life span of the filmstrip is close to expiration. The Florida Department of Education maintains an extensive online library of research, articles, and data in a project called Sunlink. A spring 1998 online article spoke of the filmstrip's demise:

> The long term prognosis for filmstrips is not good! New library media centers in the state are being supplied with audio-visual equipment that does not include filmstrip projectors. Some school districts are strongly discouraging the purchase of any filmstrips . . .
>
> It's time to start preparing yourself and your teachers for the day when filmstrips will no longer be around. Filmstrips have had a long and useful life in schools, but their time has come.
>
> You can be fairly sure that other departed media formats like vinyl records, 8-track tapes and Beta videos are all waiting on the "other side of the river" for filmstrips. We can't be positive, but we think they are now watching and waiting for the arrival of filmstrips. They know that filmstrips will be joining the audio-visual hereafter soon.[1]

Many of us can remember the shift in educational technology that took place when Sunday schools began to request television sets and videocassette recorders. The impact of television and movies on children and teenagers was so great that most Sunday school departments were eventually equipped with at least one television set and VCR.

The transition from the 16mm film projector to a television set and VCR was not always easy. Indeed, many of us experienced our first tech shock when we had to rely on our children to program the VCR. It is not that we have no experience with technology and shifts in technological requirements, it is more that change comes so fast, it leaves many feeling lost. It will be helpful to look back at some of the older technology we have used in ministry and then relate those tools to the new technology.

The Old Inventory: Tape Recorders, Film Projectors, and More

What makes for a well-equipped church office and Sunday school? Three generations of technology come to mind.

A couple of generations ago, a well-equipped church office had a secretary who could take shorthand. The office included lots of notepads, a manual typewriter, a telephone, and, if finances allowed, there was likely a Dictaphone. A church newsletter was only for wealthier churches that could afford the services of a printing press. The Sunday school relied heavily on printed curriculum.

The next generation of church offices had at least one telephone line, an electric typewriter, lots of carbon paper for making copies of correspondence, and every church secretary's dream: the mimeograph machine for producing church bulletins and newsletters! The Sunday school was equipped with a filmstrip projector, maybe a 16mm film projector with those springy wire loops that drove the spools, and a reel-to-reel tape recorder. The pace of technological change began to pick up steam in the 1960s and 1970s. Electronic stencil machines made the church secretary's job much easier. Copiers, though expensive, were available. Some warned that the price of making copies of bulletins and newsletters on a copier would be economically prohibitive, but within a decade we saw the demise of the mimeograph machine in most churches. Electric typewriters came with more functionality. Sunday school teachers enjoyed advances in the 16mm film projector. Film could be inserted into the projector, which automatically threaded the celluloid film. The overhead projector and transparencies provided a new tool for showing maps, pictures, and lesson outlines. Audiocassettes revolutionized the classroom with their availability as curriculum supplements. Some classes offered listening stations with headphones that allowed a class to hear a drama on audiocassette together.

When the time comes to invest in new technology for your church, it will be important to remember that there have always been crunch times when it was time to replace old equipment and move to the new. A new 16mm film projector was once a major investment. A film projector that cost $900.00 in 1974 would cost $3,280.83 in 1999. A copier for the office, which ran $3,500.00 in 1985, would cost $5,446.03 in 1999.[2] Having some of these figures available and recalling the financial commitment that was necessary to update in a previous generation makes one realize that finding money in the budget then was not different from the troubles we face today. In fact, when inflation is taken into account, it costs less to update technology today than it did twenty years ago.

The New Inventory: Desktops, Laptops, and LCD Projectors

As we look at new technologies, it is a good time to gain some understanding of the foundation of what people have called the "digital revolution." The new technology is not an upgrade of the old, but a genuine revolution. It is comparable in impact to the industrial revolution. It all has to do with how data or information is processed and passed on. When you write a letter to a friend, you are doing data processing; it is simply data processing using old technology. You produce information with a pen on a piece of paper by using a linear progression of letters and spaces. Then you process the information by enclosing the document in an envelope and sending it to the friend using the services of the United States Postal Service. It is a fairly old technology, but it is data processing nonetheless.[3] A typewriter is similar, but faster, technology.

Excursus

To really understand the impact of the digital revolution, we need to know the difference between analog and digital data. Analog is a way of transmitting data in alternating waves. Information is read by measuring wavelengths continuously over time. Digital data is made up of separate or discrete intervals. One of the reasons digital data is so superior to analog is seen in the difference between an audiotape or videotape and a CD or DVD. When you listen to the tape, you listen in a linear way, playing the tape from beginning to end. It is possible to skip the tape ahead, but the search process can be frustrating. Because of the way the data is put together on a CD or DVD, it is possible to go to the specific track or scene. Digital data is addressable. Remember those old computers with the large tape drives (you've likely seen them in old television programs or movies) and twelve-inch reels of tape? The tapes would go round and round in a jerky kind of way as the computer read the data. The data had to be read in a linear way from beginning to end. Sorting data took a long time as the computer worked to reorganize the data on the tapes. Because digital data is randomly accessible (in addition to the fact that computers are lightning fast in comparison), a two-hour sort in 1970 takes a second or two today. The most important difference between digital and analog data is that the quality and reliability of digital data are superior and do not degrade over time. The merging of technologies, like the integration of the cell phone and Internet, is possible because of digital data. The cell phone is able to portray Internet information on a tiny screen because it can produce digital data as sound or video. All the files on your computer are stored in digital format. These files can be documents, pictures, or sounds.

When you walk into a local church office that has kept pace with changing technologies, you will see a computer on the secretary's desk where the typewriter once sat. If the secretary is working full-time, there are two telephone lines available. One is a standard telephone line and the second is for email and Internet access. The congregation obtained email and Internet access about a year ago and most of the newsletters, committee minutes, and bulletin information is sent to the office as email attachments. The pastor and secretary are able to share the line that is used for email and Internet access, and there is a third line for the pastor's office.

The copier in the church office is a heavy-duty copier used to produce the worship bulletin and church newsletter as well as materials for the Sunday school classes. The church decided on the heavy-duty copier when the Sunday school classes began using materials and lessons that are available on the Internet and which include permission to copy for local church use.[4] The church board is considering the idea of building money into the budget for a leased copier since the current copier's usage has been at least double what was expected.

A multifunction printer sits near the computer. It is used by the computer as a printer, serves as a light-duty copier, and is also the church's fax machine. The church board is considering a high-end printer down the road, but for the time being the multifunction printer is the most economical way to address the need for a printer and fax machine.

The latest addition to the church office is a laptop computer and an LCD projector. The congregation decided to keep these in the church's central office since they are used during worship, in the Sunday school classes, and by committees and study groups. The laptop computer and LCD projector are used together to show PowerPoint presentations, lesson plans, announcements, and short video clips. The LCD projector is able to project signals from a VCR or DVD as well as the laptop computer. Requests to use the LCD projector came in once or twice a week when it was first purchased a few months ago, but as more people learned what the laptop and LCD projector could do, requests skyrocketed. People began to consider the possibilities when the youth group's Web site was shown to the Christian Education Committee by bringing the site up on the laptop computer and projecting through the LCD to a screen in the boardroom.

The Sunday school classes also have a computer with email and Internet access available. Classes have been in touch with missionaries through email and use the Internet access to take virtual tours of countries where the church has mission interests. Plans are being developed to include Internet access and Sunday school software in the church's curriculum budget.

As technology use in several areas of the church increased, the church board appointed a team of persons to develop an overall plan for integrating technology into the congregation's mission.

What to Replace and When to Replace It

As your church moves into the area of planning and purchasing equipment, keep in mind that there are two essential components to planning for technology. The first is systems analysis. Systems analysis is a complete and broad-based examination of your church's structure and ministry goals. What possibilities are there for technology use in each area of our church life? What impact will the Internet and new technologies have on our church and its members? What kinds of resources—in terms of finances and personnel—are available? How much will expenditures for the new be covered by eliminating some expenses from the old?

The second component in planning is programming. What departments of our church will be involved in any decisions that are made with respect to technology? Who should be a part of our discussion? How do we plan to integrate the technology with our current programs, and in what order should that happen?

I offer more information on administration and planning in part 4, but the factors mentioned above will help as you consider replacing old equipment with new. One of the great things about current technological trends is that the cost of personal and small-business computing has dropped radically in the past few years. My earlier figures showed that the cost of getting up to speed with essential equipment for use in ministry is actually less than the cost of equipment a generation ago. A bonus in all of this is that today you get more functionality as well as lower prices. Here are some basic principles to consider when replacing equipment.

- *Replace your typewriter.* If you are still without a basic desktop computer for your church, the first thing to do is purchase a computer to replace the typewriter. An efficient new typewriter would cost between $700 and $1,000. An entry-level computer would cost about the same.
- *Replace your computer.* I know this sounds strange, but if you are working with anything less than a Pentium III computer processor (or equivalent) with less than 64 MB of RAM, you should replace the computer. Your computer is your data and information processor and your doorway to the wider world. A good rule of thumb is to anticipate using your computer twice as much as you originally planned.
- *Replace your phone line.* Well, not *replace* actually, but upgrade. Set up an account with an ISP and get connected to the Internet. Email and Internet access will become the basic tools in your ministry. If you can afford it, you should seriously consider adding a second telephone line if you currently have only one. Between email and Internet use and with the possibility of the pastor using the Internet for study and research, the demands on one phone line will create some frustration with people who may be trying to reach the church office. An alter-

native is to get voice mail that is able to take messages when the phone line is busy. An answering machine does not do any good when the line is busy. Consider the voice mail alternative only if economics make a second phone line prohibitive.

After you have completed these three basic steps in replacing old technology, or perhaps more accurately, become equipped to begin, it is time to move ahead.

- *Replace your 16mm film projector and television set with an LCD projector.* The LCD projector will become the central audiovisual tool in your ministry *and* it will be the most expensive. They are currently available anywhere from $2,900 and up. Plan to do some careful research when you begin shopping for an LCD projector. How you plan to use the projector will determine the requirements and price.[5]
- *Better yet, replace your 16mm film projector, television set, slide projector, overhead projector,* and *television set with an LCD projector and laptop computer.* When you do a side-by-side comparison of the real cost of these items, the newer technology is a bargain.

Once you have purchased a computer and have thought through some of the ways you will be using the new technologies in your church's ministry, it is time to move further into using software. My aim now is to move from some of the theory and foundations we have been exploring to practical application.

Chapter Seven
More About Software: PowerPoint

There are two essential software tools (programs) you will need to become familiar with when you begin implementing new programs in your ministry. The first is presentation software, which is software that can produce presentations for worship, Sunday school classes, adult studies, and committee meetings. Presentation software produces slides. However, these are not your mother's slides. These slides include colors, sounds, and animations that bring life to your presentation. The second program we will explore is the software you will need to create a Web page.

You will have choices about which software to use for both producing slides and authoring Web pages. As you continue developing your skills in using new tools for ministry, you will be able to decide which software tools you want to use. For these purposes, however, I will focus on the PowerPoint presentation graphics program and the FrontPage Express Web site creation and management tool. PowerPoint and FrontPage Express are easy to learn and work well with all other Microsoft products. This does not mean I believe Microsoft software for these tasks is superior to all others. As a matter of fact, there are some other wonderful products available for creating Web pages. If you become a Web page designer, there are a number of choices that many designers prefer other than FrontPage.[1] (FrontPage Express is the free version of the Microsoft FrontPage Web site creation and management tool.) FrontPage

Express is a "lite" version of FrontPage and is given away by Microsoft with the idea that transition to FrontPage will be smooth. PowerPoint, on the other hand, has become a standard for presentation software.

Once you have begun using some of these tools in your ministry, one of your considerations will be how well your intended audience can use the materials you produce. You will want your Web page viewers to see your pages clearly and those who use your presentations to do so without difficulty. One of the reasons I use the Microsoft suite of products is that the majority of computer users are able to access the materials produced by PowerPoint and FrontPage. When you are ready to begin working with PowerPoint and FrontPage you will need to obtain the software programs and install them on your computer. Remember that you can start out with FrontPage Express, which is free to use. There are more instructions in chapter 8. You can buy these programs where you purchased your computer, but they may be available through your denominational connections at a substantially reduced price. United Methodists, for instance, can purchase Microsoft Office®* products through the denomination below standard retail price.

What PowerPoint Is and What It Can Do

Creating a presentation with PowerPoint is nothing more than a computerized way of doing a slide presentation. You could say that PowerPoint is to slides what word processing is to typing.

With the old typewriter technology, you would type on a sheet of paper. If you made a mistake, you could use correction fluid on the mistake, backspace, and correct the mistake. Then came a leap in technology. Advanced typewriters were equipped with correction tape. Now you could backspace, cover over the mistake, and type a correction in a couple of easy moves. However, there were many limitations. If you made too many mistakes you had to toss the sheet

---

* Microsoft Office® is either a registered trademark or trademark of Microsoft Corporation in the United States and/or other countries.

and start over. Some of us remember those times when we discovered mistakes in a document after removing it from the typewriter. We would reinsert the sheet and attempt to get the sheet lined up so that we could avoid having to do the whole page over again.

Word processing came along to make life so much easier for people who did a lot of typing. Now it was possible to correct mistakes, move paragraphs, and change the size and style of the type. These capabilities were exceptionally helpful when a letter that was just a little bit too long to fit on one page could be instantly made to fit. There were some who resisted the introduction of word processing because it meant learning to use a computer. I asked my secretary what she would do if she had to go back to a typewriter to do her work each day. "I would quit," she said.

I countered, "And what did you think when they first asked you to switch from a typewriter to word processing on a computer?"

"I wanted to quit!" she answered.

PowerPoint is a way to create slides using the computer. Unlike slides you create with a camera, you can change colors, add text, remove text, and have animated text and pictures appear on your slide. The slides you created with your camera were once shown on a screen through a slide projector. The slides you create with PowerPoint can be shown on your computer screen, projected on a screen with an LCD projector, and uploaded to a Web site.

Just as a word processor can produce documents that can be used in many different ways (Sunday bulletins, letters, and booklets to name a few), so also Power Point can be used to prepare lessons for Sunday school, supplementary materials for worship, and outlines, graphs, and charts for committee meetings.

Building Your First Presentation

In this section, I will present the basic steps of creating a PowerPoint presentation. To begin, open this program on your computer and follow these directions to begin working on your first presentation.

1. When you first open the program, you will see this screen:

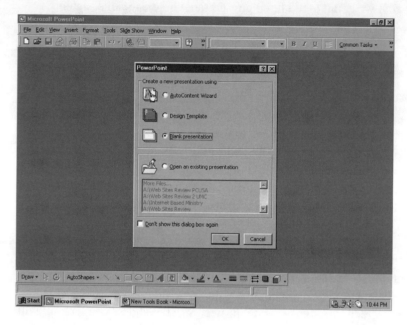

Figure 7a

You will notice that the screen looks similar to other Microsoft products. One of the advantages to using PowerPoint is that the look and feel of the program are very similar to other Microsoft word processing and Web page programs.

2. This screen gives you three choices for putting together a presentation. The Auto Content Wizard guides you through various ways to organize and give style to your presentation. The second choice is to use a Design Template, which automatically gives all of your slides a consistent format of colors and type styles. These will be helpful when you gain some experience in preparing presentations and want to quickly apply a look and feel to your project. For now, we will us the Blank Presentation method. When you learn to use the basic PowerPoint tools, it will be much easier to use some

of the automatic functions like design templates and the auto content wizard. Go ahead and click OK to begin building a presentation.

3. The screen you come to offers several options for preparing a slide. There are twelve types of layouts available. These represent the way your slide will look when projected. You will notice that you can use charts, photographs, images, organizational charts, and more when creating a slide.

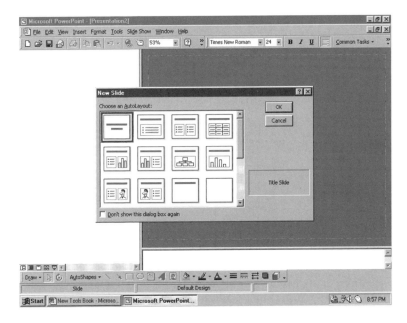

Figure 7b

For our purposes, the blank slide will provide the best opportunity for learning the essential parts of creating a slide. Click on the bottom-right blank slide and then click OK.

4. The next screen brings us to the basic view in this program, where all the essential functions are available and the work of creating a slide is done. Keep this slide view open while going through the outline and exercises that follow the diagram.

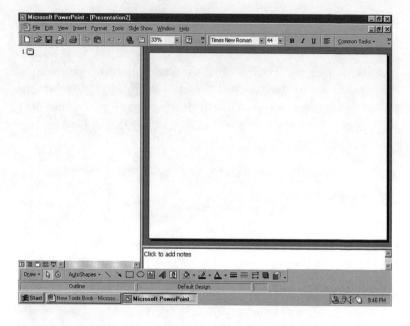

Figure 7c

Hint: I recommend that you do the following exercises in order when you have time to complete them all at once. Allow yourself about an hour to do this. You may want to go through these exercises more than once to become familiar and comfortable with using the program. If you find it necessary to leave the exercises before you can finish them, read through the steps beginning with exercise one to refresh your memory as you continue your project.

EXERCISE ONE: THE MOUSE BUTTONS

This exercise is not limited to PowerPoint, but will apply to using your mouse in any program. The mouse has a left button and a right button. Think of the right button as asking the question "What can I do?" When you click the right button in any area of the screen in any of your programs, a menu will appear that tells what can be done in this particular area of the screen. The left button issues a command that says, "Do this." Go ahead and move around your open PowerPoint screen, including the menu bar and taskbar at the bottom of the page, then click the right mouse button. Each area of the screen will give a different menu. Don't apply any of the commands by clicking the left mouse button at this point; simply take some time to explore the screen. As we move through the various functions in creating a slide, the right mouse button will frequently provide a shortcut to many of the tasks you want to accomplish.

EXERCISE TWO: YOUR VERY FIRST SLIDES

The left side of the screen, with the number "1" and an icon resembling a small slide, is an outline of your slide presentation. There is only one slide on your outline, but as you create more slides, they will show up as slide "2," "3," and so on. Try this now by clicking on the menu option Insert. It is the fourth option from the left, located at the top of the screen on the menu bar where you will find File, Edit, View, and Insert. The very first option you will see is New Slide with the small icon of a slide. Click the New Slide command and a box will appear as it did in Figure 7b. The slide layout choice will default to the blank slide that you chose earlier. Now click OK.

Now you have two slides you can work on in your program. The second slide will appear beneath slide 1 on the left side. There is nothing on these slides at this point. You could continue to add slides, which may be helpful if you know ahead of time how many slides you want to use in your presentation. There is a shortcut to adding slides to your program. Just below the menu bar, there is another toolbar with icons on it. It looks like this:

Figure 7d

These small icons are shortcuts to the menu items. When you move your mouse pointer to one of the icons and let it sit for a couple of seconds, without clicking the mouse, text will appear that tells you what the icon does. Notice in the diagram what the new slide icon looks like. In this diagram, the mouse has been placed on the New Slide icon.

Click the New Slide icon and then choose OK to add slide 3. Do this two more times to create a slide program of five slides. You will see the five slides on the left side of the screen in the program outline.

EXERCISE THREE: HOW TO UNDO MISTAKES

One of the most important buttons in the Microsoft suite of programs is the Undo button. Underneath the Tools option on the menu bar there is a small blue arrow that curls back to the left. When you click on this Undo arrow, the last function you performed in the program will be undone. Go ahead and click the Undo arrow. You will notice that the last slide you inserted will be deleted. Click the Undo button three more times and you will be back at the first slide.

What happens if you mistakenly undo a part of your work? In other words you want to redo an action. The menu bar that shows the icons also has a Redo arrow that curls to the right. If this Redo arrow is not visible, click the small double arrows (>>) just to the right of the question mark. The Redo arrow will appear in the group of icons that you see. Click the Redo arrow four times and the five slides will return.

EXERCISE FOUR: CREATE YOUR SLIDES

In the outline of your slides on the left side of the screen, click slide number 1. The first thing we will do is to create a color for our slides. On the menu bar, click the option Format. Now go down and click the option Background. A small box will appear called Background. Underneath the "Background fill" box there is a small blank box with an arrow facing down. Click the arrow and you will have the opportunity to choose More Colors or Fill Effects. Choose More Colors and then pick a color for the background of your slides by clicking in the color palette. When you have picked a color, choose OK and then Apply to All. All of your slides will have the color you chose as the background for every slide. If you had chosen Apply, the color would have been applied to only the slide you were working on.

Congratulations! You have just created a five-slide presentation in PowerPoint. This is all there is to it! The only problem is—don't be insulted now—your presentation is quite dull. It contains five slides, all the same color, and there is no other content.

Before we continue with the exercises there is a critical issue you need to understand that will help you with *any* computer work. *"Save Your Work!"* If for any reason your computer should experience a power outage, program malfunction, or if you inadvertently exit your program without saving your file, you could lose a lot of work. One of the awful cries heard round the world in scores of languages is the cry of someone who has spent an afternoon working on a computer program only to lose his work. Even expert users have times when the failure to obey the "save your work" principle results in pain and anguish.

Save your presentation by choosing the File menu option and then Save As when the submenu appears. The following Save As box will appear. Follow the steps in the diagram and save your work:

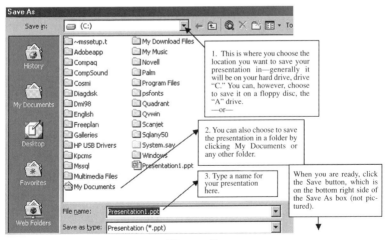

Figure 7e

Another important note about saving your work: Your series of slides is a single presentation. When you save a presentation, you are saving all the slides associated with it.

EXERCISE FIVE: WORKING WITH TEXT

A presentation needs more than five colored slides. At a minimum, you should have some text on your slides. With your first slide still selected, go once again to the menu options and choose Insert. Then choose Text Box from the menu that drops down. Now click in the large area on the right side of the screen. A small box will appear and your cursor will be inside the box. Type something like "My Slide Presentation" in the box. Now you have a slide with some text. The next step is to work with your text to achieve different effects. Select your text. (Click and hold the left mouse button at the beginning of the text and drag the cursor over the text until the text is highlighted.) Now go to the Format option on your menu bar and click it. A sub-menu will appear with Font as the very first option. Click Font and a box called a dialog box will appear with other effects.

You can explore the font dialog box to try out various functions available in this part of your program. Keep in mind that you can use your Undo arrow to reverse changes to your text and try some others.

When you are ready to proceed, change the type size to 48. Notice that the text box is surrounded by slashes or dots to indicate the text box boundary. There are also eight tiny boxes that look like this: ☐. The boxes are called "handles" because you can click and hold on them to manipulate the size of the box. When you put your cursor in the area of the small boxes, or handles, you will see a double arrow that looks something like this: ↔. When you click and hold the box, you can change its size by dragging the arrow. Let go of the left mouse button when you are satisfied with the size of the box. Take some time to practice changing the size of the box.

Now put your cursor on the text box boundary indicated by the dots or slashes that outline the text box. A symbol made up of four small arrows will appear. When you click and hold the text box boundaries with the left mouse button, you can move the box with its text to any position on the page. Release the left mouse button when you are satisfied with the position of the box on your slide. Now you can insert text on a page, change the size of the text, and place the text anywhere on the slide you would like to have it appear. Take some time to work with your text by changing the style and size of the text and its position on the page.

One last thing we want to do before adding text to your four remaining slides is to add some color to the text. Select the text on your slide as you did earlier when you made the size changes. (Click and hold the left mouse button at the beginning of the text and drag the cursor over the text until the text is highlighted.) From the menu options at the top of the page, choose Format and then Font from the menu that appears. The font dialog box will again appear, which allows you to change the style, size, and color of the text, as well as a few other functions. For our purposes, we want to find Color (on the right side of the box); click the down arrow and choose More Colors. From the color palette that appears, click the color you want for your text and then choose OK. This is another good place to explore a few more things you can do with your text. Remember that you need to highlight your text before you can make changes to it. Try various colors and experiment with adding shadow to the text. Check the box beside Shadow on the lower left side of the Font dialog box beneath the section called Effects.

Now that you have added text to your first slide, it is time to add text to the four remaining slides in your program. Click slide 2 on the left side of the screen. The large area that represents the slide you are working on will be the work area for slide 2. This slide is the same color as the first slide, but needs text added. Following the instructions for adding text to the first slide, go ahead and add text to each page, size the text, and choose the colors. Your slides could give an outline of a lesson you are planning to use in a class, an agenda for a committee meeting, a sermon outline, or an outline for a training event.

When you have finished adding text to all five slides, you have completed your PowerPoint presentation. There is much more that you can learn with PowerPoint. It is a powerful program with capabilities that will take some time and practice to learn.

EXERCISE SIX:
VIEWING YOUR SHOW

The first thing we want to do when we have created something is to look over our accomplishment. This has biblical foundations; it goes back to the beginning of creation. Even God stopped to take in what had been done in six days: "God saw everything that he had made, and indeed, it was very good" (Genesis 1:31). It is time to take a look at the slide presentation you have made.

On the menu options at the top of your page, go to the seventh item called Slide Show. When you click Slide Show, another menu will appear and you will choose the first option, View Show. A full-screen representation of your first slide will appear. You advance through your slides by clicking the left mouse button. When you get to the last screen, go ahead and click the left mouse button and you will be taken back to the basic screen of the program.

Voilà! You've created and presented a PowerPoint slide presentation. If your computer were connected to an LCD projector, you could show your presentation to a group.

EXERCISE SEVEN:
ADDING SPARKLE

Background and text can be effective tools for presenting a lesson plan, but there is much more you can accomplish with presentation software.

We will first add a graphic to slide 1. Be sure you click slide 1 on the left side of the page where your slides are listed. Go to the fourth menu option at the top of your screen and choose Insert. When the next menu appears, click Picture. Several choices will appear. This is where you can insert a digital photograph or scanned photo you may have on a floppy disc. As you develop skill in using Power-Point, you will be able to create powerful presentations using all the available functions. For now, click Picture, then Clip Art. When you choose Clip Art, you will see something like the following screen:

Figure 7f

You can come back to this screen later and explore all the functions that are available. Looking at the top of the screen, you will see that you can import clips (namely take photos or scanned items and add them to the clips available to you when creating slides), or you can connect to the Internet and find clips that Microsoft has made available in its art library that is available on the PowerPoint support site.[2]

Choose the category Buildings and then pick one of the pictures for your page by clicking it. When you click the picture you want, a small box will appear that represents four options for using the picture. You will choose the top option, which is a small icon representing Insert Picture. Click this icon and then close the clip art box by clicking the small X at the upper right-hand corner of the clip art box to close the window. The picture you have chosen will be inserted on your slide.

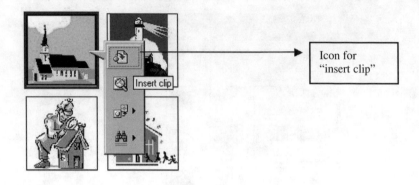

Figure 7g

This would be a good location to place your text and picture on the slide. When you click and hold the left mouse button inside the picture on your slide, you will be able to drag the picture to any position you desire on the slide. Click anywhere on your text and the text box will appear. Remember that you can click and hold your left mouse button on the slashes in the box and move the text to various locations on the slide. This will become an important design tool when you create presentations.

Take time to practice adding pictures to your other slides. When you have time, come back and work with the colors, pictures, text sizes, and placement of items on the page. This will help you gain familiarity with the many tools that are available for creating exciting presentations. As you work, remember to go back to Slide Show on the menu bar and choose View Show to go through your presentation as you develop it. This will help you get a sense of how the program is developing from your audience's perspective.

There is another menu option you will want to use to reach shortcuts to the more common tasks in PowerPoint. Click the menu option View at the top of your page and then move down to Toolbars. It will look like this:

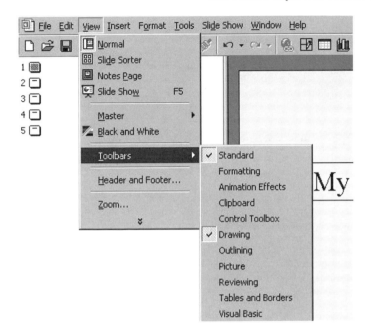

Figure 7h

The standard and drawing toolbars are checked in this diagram. These two, along with the formatting toolbar, are the most commonly used and the ones you will use as you begin working with PowerPoint. If the drawing toolbar is not checked on your screen, check it now. Note that the appearance of submenus—like the one pictured here that appears when you move your mouse down to Toolbars—can be a bit slippery when you move the cursor to the option you would like to choose. (If the submenu appears and then disappears, it is simply because you moved the cursor off the submenu. Try again and with a bit of practice you will fine-tune your ability to use the mouse.)

There is one more part of the program you will use regularly. At the bottom left of your screen there are five tiny icons that are shortcuts to viewing your slide presentation. They look like this:

Figure 7i

The first icon represents the Normal View of the presentation that you have been working with. After the Normal View, the next icon to the right represents the Outline View of your presentation. Then follow the Slide, Slide Sorter, and Slide Show views. Try clicking each of these views to get a sense of what they do. The Slide View icon, for instance, will display a view of your slide as it will project it during presentation. Use the Escape button on your keyboard to return to the normal view. (It's the "Esc" key near the top left of your keyboard.) The Slide View gives you a larger representation of the slide that you may find useful for working on your individual slides. The Slide Sorter View is especially helpful when you want to see the whole presentation. As the name suggests, you can also use this to sort your slides. It is just like the old 35mm slide sorters in which you would lay out your slides and move them around as you wanted to project them. With this slide sorter, you simply click with the left mouse button on one of the slides and hold the left mouse button down while you drag it to the new position. (This is called "click and hold.") Give this a try by moving your slides around.

EXERCISE EIGHT: MORE SPARKLE

Now it is time to add a bit more sparkle to your program by using the Drawing toolbar you turned on earlier. (It is possible your program came with the Drawing toolbar already selected.)

Go to your first slide and work on it in the Slide View. Click the Slide View icon I just discussed. On the left side of your screen you can still select which slide you would like to work on even though you are now in Slide View. Click slide 1 on the left side of your screen.

Move your mouse across the Drawing toolbar, allowing the cursor to settle on each item until the text appears that tells you what the item is. For this exercise, click the blue, slanted "A" at the bottom of the screen. The WordArt Gallery will appear where you can choose from thirty different styles of text. Choose one and click OK. Now you can choose a text style (B for bold text and *I* for italic text) and size. Highlight Your Text Here and type your text—something like "My Zippy Text"—then choose the style and size. Now choose OK and you will have added more sparkle to your slide. You will be able to click and hold your new text to move it around the slide, and change the size by holding and dragging the handles. When you have time to experiment with the various text styles and possibilities using this function, you will begin to have some real fun with the program.

We will look at two more functions available on the Drawing toolbar and then I will ask you to experiment with the other functions to gain confidence with the program.

First of all, try the small icon that represents the text box. It has the small "A" on a tiny page. Click the icon and then click anywhere in the area of your slide. This is a shortcut to inserting a text box on your page. Practice adding text to one or more of your slides. Large text is used for titles. Smaller text can represent subpoints. Remember that when your slide is projected for an audience, the text must be large enough for all to see. Text should be no smaller than 24 points for group presentations. The tiny icon of a man's picture two places to the right of the text box icon is a shortcut to inserting a picture on your slide. Try inserting a picture on one or two of your slides.

The left end of your drawing toolbar gives you the opportunity to add lines, boxes, and ovals. The little down arrow just to the right of the Auto Shapes text offers some attention-getting shapes and images to add to your slides. Experiment with a few of these functions. (Remember that all-important Undo button while you experiment!)

From this point you should be able to explore the various functions of PowerPoint and be ready to give a presentation within a week or ten days that will impress your audience. There is one more exercise I want to lead you through before I turn you loose on the program as you prepare for your first audience.

EXERCISE NINE: EXTREME SPARKLE

Now comes the part of PowerPoint that makes your presentations so much more than a slide show. If you have added text and pictures to all five of your slides, add a new slide to your presentation. (You remember how to do this, right? *Hint:* Click the New Slide icon.) Now click the Text Box icon on the drawing toolbar (the box with lines and the small "A") and click inside your new slide. Type "Point Number One," then add another text box and type "Point Number Two." Make any size, style, and color changes you desire to the text.

Click "Point Number One" to activate the text box. Here's the key part to this exercise. Click the right mouse button inside the text box. The menu that appears will look like this:

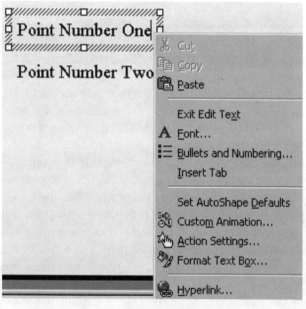

Figure 7j

Choose custom animation and you will see a box like the following. You can animate any of the items in your slide by checking the box that represents the text (or picture). When you check a box, the corresponding text or picture will show the box around it. This means you will be applying an effect to that item.

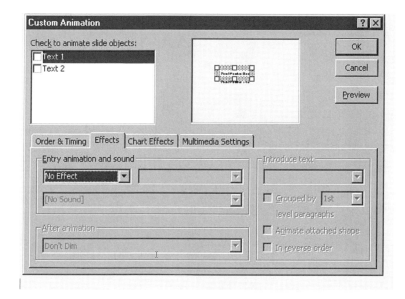

Figure 7k

Now follow this procedure:

1. Choose the Effects Tab if it is not already selected.
2. Check the box that says "Text 1." When you click a check box, the text represented by that box will be highlighted in the window to the right of the check boxes.

The Custom Animation dialog box will now appear something like this:

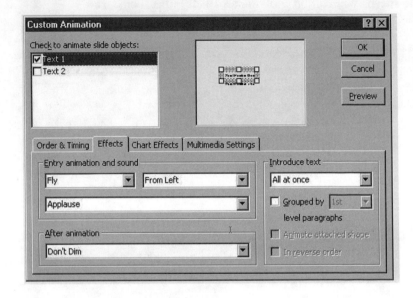

Figure 7l

1. Choose the way you want your text to enter the slide.
2. Choose which direction you would like the text to enter your slide.
3. Choose a sound you would like to associate with the text entry.

Now click the box for "Text 2" and follow the same steps to apply effects to the second text box. Finally, click OK near the top right of the dialog box.

Now click the Slide Show icon on the lower left side of your screen. Your slide will show up on the screen. Click the left mouse button to advance the various items on your slide. To watch your entire slide show, click the Slide Show option and then choose View Show. Click the left mouse button to advance the slides.

Now you can *really* begin to have some fun. As you practice using the "Custom Animation" effects, you can apply the effects to pictures as well as text. Try this with some of your clip art and photos.

There is much more that you can do with PowerPoint. It is a very powerful program with functionality we have not even begun to explore. As you use the things you have learned, you will become more comfortable working with and exploring other features of this program. The companion Web site will contain links to tutorials and other resources for PowerPoint.

Chapter Eight

More About Software:
Creating a Web Presence

This chapter will concentrate on the mechanics of creating a Web presence for your church. I will discuss administrative and planning tasks associated with creating a Web site for the church in chapter 9.

A Web Presence for Your Church
in Four Hours or Less

The quickest and easiest way to put up a Web site for your church is to use a free service such as the one provided by the American Bible Society on its Web site, *www.forministry.com.* When you visit this Web site, you will find a link to an area where you can register as an editor for your church and have a site up and running in four hours or less. There are a number of sites where you can build a Web site for free, but most of them come with heavy advertising on the pages people view. Some of these services will be listed on the companion Web site, but the forministry.com service is currently the finest free service I know of.

There are advantages to using a service such as forministry.com. The task of creating HTML code that can be read by browsers is done for you by the service. You simply add text to templates that are professionally designed, and the site is hosted for free on the "For Ministry" server. One of the ways some people become acquainted with creating a Web site is to use one of the free services while using the Web site tools and becoming more familiar with creating a Web site. The site is not advertised or made public while the development and learning take place. A team of two or three people could use the free service and work with the administrative and planning ideas offered in chapter 9. This will give you a sense of how an Internet site works, what can be done with it, and the kind of work that is involved in creating a Web site.

There are also some disadvantages to using a free service. There are limitations to the functionality of a free site. You cannot use forms, submit registrations, create prayer forums, have a photographic virtual tour of the church, or accomplish many other interactive functions. A second disadvantage is that the address of your Internet site (the URL) will be long and difficult for people to remember. Visitors are not as likely to visit a church site when they have to write down a URL and type a cumbersome address into the browser address bar. If you were to develop a Web site for your church at *www.forministry.com,* for instance, your church's Internet address would be something like *www.forministry.com/12345UPC.*

A Web Presence for Your Church in More Than Four Hours

Churches that plan to use the Internet in their ministries will need the flexibility that comes with writing and publishing their own Web pages. Web site design, publishing, and maintenance require the investment of time and have a higher learning curve than PowerPoint. Nevertheless, understanding the basics of Web site creation and publication is *not* difficult, and it will be helpful to have a number of people in your church who understand these basics. Creating your own Web site will take more than four hours, but the investment of time and energy in doing this will provide a great foundation for a new form of ministry. This chapter will provide a simple overview of the whole process, including the creation of Web pages using FrontPage Express. I will discuss the administrative and planning tasks that are required in effective Web ministry in chapter 10.

For now, let's take a look at the three basic steps required to create and publish a Web site:

1. Pick a software program for writing Web (HTML) pages.
2. Learn to use the software.
3. Publish your Web site.

PICK A SOFTWARE PROGRAM FOR WRITING WEB PAGES

In chapter 2, I discussed briefly the fact that Web pages are written in a code called HTML (hypertext markup language). The beginning code for our Web site at the University of Dubuque Theological Seminary looks like this:

```
<html>
<head>
<TITLE>University of Dubuque Theological Seminary.
Preparing compassionate, competent local church
pastors.</TITLE>

<META NAME="description" CONTENT="The University of
Dubuque Theological Seminary is a seminary of the
Presbyterian Church (USA) with a focus on preparation of car-
ing, compassionate and committed local church pastors.">
<META NAME="keywords" CONTENT="seminary, seminary
education, theological education, theology, presbyterian semi-
naries, methodist, continuing education, lay ministry, iowa,
dubuque, 52001, M.Div, MAR">
<meta http-equiv="Content-Language" content="en-us">
<meta http-equiv="Content-Type" content="text/html;
charset=windows-1252">
<meta name="GENERATOR" content="Microsoft FrontPage
4.0">
<meta name="ProgId" content="FrontPage.Editor.Document">
<title>welcome</title>
```

It is possible to write your entire Web site using HTML with a simple text editor. Chances are you have neither the desire nor the time to learn how to code Web pages using HTML. The good news is that anyone can publish a Web page without knowing how to write HTML. It should be said, however, that it is helpful for people who will be involved in working with Web sites to know something about HTML.[1]

There are many software programs available that write the HTML code for you. I've mentioned Microsoft FrontPage. As your church develops a Web ministry, your Web ministry team can decide the issue of which software will best meet your needs.

LEARN TO USE THE SOFTWARE

We will use a program called Microsoft FrontPage Express for the purposes of this brief tutorial. FrontPage Express is a simple version of FrontPage. There are three reasons for this choice. The most obvious reason is that the program is free. It comes with Microsoft Internet Explorer version 4.0 and above. Second, the look and feel of the program are quite similar to the word processor program, Microsoft Word, which makes it easier to transfer one's knowledge between Microsoft programs. Third, the transition from FrontPage Express to the more powerful FrontPage is easy to accomplish.

Here are the steps to creating a Web page with FrontPage Express:

1. Locate FrontPage Express on Your Computer
(This tutorial will only work if you have Microsoft Internet Explorer 4.0 or above installed on your computer.)

Click the Start button and a menu will appear. Scroll up to Programs where another menu will appear. Now scroll to Internet Explorer where yet another menu will appear. Now choose FrontPage Express. See Figure 8a. Note that the only difference between Figure 8a and what you'll need to do will be moving your cursor to Internet Explorer instead of Accessories.

If you have Microsoft Windows 98, second edition, the FrontPage Express program may be located in another folder. Click Start then Programs. Now choose Accessories then Internet Tools and finally FrontPage Express.

Figure 8a

If you are not able to locate FrontPage Express on your computer, you can download a copy from a link on the companion Web site. Visit *www.newtools-online.com* and choose Resources. From there you will find a link to an Internet site where you may download the program.[2]

2. Open FrontPage Express by Clicking the Icon
   When you open the program the screen will look like this:

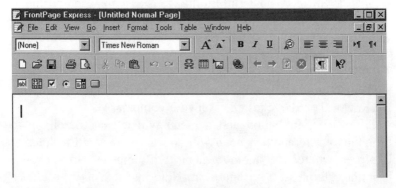

Figure 8b

If the screen area of your page is gray, go to the menu option File at the top of the page, then choose Page Properties. A Page Properties dialog box will be displayed. Click the Background tab and you will see the following box:

Figure 8c

Click the small arrow beside the background box and then choose White. Finally, click OK at the bottom of the box. Now your screen will appear as white and your page will be much easier to see. You are now ready to begin creating your Web page.

3. Building Your First Web Page

As you begin working with FrontPage Express, you will notice that many of the things you learned in using PowerPoint will apply now. The menu items at the top of your page are similar, and by clicking the various menu options, you will be able to see the functions that are available to you. Click the menu option View and you will see which toolbars are turned on and which are turned off.

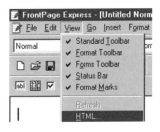

Figure 8d

Take a moment to click the various toolbars and then notice which functions are available when the toolbars are turned on and off. For this exercise, we will be using the Standard and Format toolbars.

4. Adding Text to Your Page

Now look at the formatting toolbar in Figure 8b. It is the toolbar right under the menu items. Near the right-hand end of the toolbar, there are three small sets of lines. Bring your mouse to rest over each set of lines and wait a moment. The text for each icon will appear. When you click one of these icons, your text will be aligned to the left (the default setting for text), centered, or aligned to the right. Click the icon for centering text and your cursor will be placed at the center of the page.

Type some text along the line of "First Church Web Page." (In all these examples, you should type the suggested text without the quote marks.)

Congratulations! You have just created your first Web page. Would you like to see the HTML code you have just created? Click the View menu option and then choose HTML. Now your page will display the HTML code you have just written. (Well, actually FrontPage Express wrote the code, but you told the program what code to write.) Your code looks something like this:

```
: View or Edit HTML

<html>

<head>
<meta http-equiv="Content-Type"
content="text/html; charset=iso-8859-1">
<meta name="GENERATOR" content="Microsoft FrontPage Express 2.0">
<title>Untitled Normal Page</title>
</head>

<body bgcolor="#FFFFFF">

<p align="center"><font size="3">First Church Web Page</font></p>
</body>
</html>
```

Figure 8e

Get ready to write your own HTML code! On your FrontPage Express screen, go down to the eighth line where the code says <body bgcolor = "#FFFFFF">. This code is telling the browser to show the background of the page as white. Replace the FFFFFF with A3D3F3. Go to the next line and replace the text "First Church Web Page" with "St. John's Web Page" (without the quotes). Now click OK at the bottom on the View or Edit HTML dialog box.

More congratulations are in order. You have successfully created a Web page and made some behind-the-scenes changes to the HTML code. It is possible to learn HTML and write your complete page in HTML. For most of us, however, programs like FrontPage Express are wonderful.

It is helpful to have some knowledge of HTML simply to understand what is happening when you create a Web page and for those times when the people who are writing and maintaining a Web site will find it easier to go in and tweak the code to correct errors rather than waiting for someone else to do it.

Take a few moments now to explore the functions of your formatting toolbar. Highlight the text on your page and experiment with changing the size of the text. The large "A" on the formatting toolbar with the up arrow will increase the size of the text. The small "a" with the down arrow will decrease the text size. Choose the small icon that looks like a painter's pallet with a small "a" beside it to change the color of your text. (This icon is the fifth icon to the right of your Increase Text icon.) When you change the color of your text, you will need to click anywhere on your screen to deselect your text. This will allow you to see the new color of the text.

Another way to work with your text and the background colors of the page is to click the Format menu option at the top of the page and then choose Background. Here you can choose the background color of the page and the text. As you experiment with changes in the look and feel of your Web page, you can use the View and HTML menu items to see how the code is changing. One of the ways to learn more about HTML is to view the code as you create pages and see how it relates to what actually appears on the page.

The companion Web site *(www.newtools-online.com)* will have links to tutorials on HTML for those who wish to dig a little deeper into using it. (Remember to click OK to exit the View or Edit HTML box to get back to your page.)

There is one more exercise to do with your text. Adding text to your page will be similar to adding text in any word processing program. Look at your screen once again. Place the cursor at the end of your title, "St. John's Web Page," and then add the words "Church History." Choose Enter again and add "Worship Times." Finally, add one more line of text: "Meeting Times." We want the three lines that were just added to be subheadings under the title. It would improve the look of the page if we could reduce the size of the text a bit and turn the three items into a bulleted list. Select the text of these three lines by placing your cursor at the beginning of "Church History." Now hold the left mouse button down as you drag the cursor to the end of the third line. Release the left mouse button when the text has been selected.

Figure 8f

On the formatting toolbar, choose the icon for decreasing the text and click twice to make the text smaller. Now choose the Format menu option at the top of the page and then click Bullets and Numbering. The List Properties dialog box will appear. The first tab, Bulleted, has four choices represented by the four boxes. The top right choice outlined in blue is the current choice. This choice is actually "no bullets" for the list. Choose any of the remaining three boxes and then choose OK to see your page. Select any of the styles you desire in the List Properties dialog box and then choose OK at the bottom of the box to see the changes you have made. (Remember to deselect the highlighted text by clicking anywhere on the screen so that you can see your changes.) If you wanted a numbered list instead of a bulleted list, you would highlight the text and choose Format and Bullets and Numbering again. This time you would choose the Numbered tab and pick one of the numbering styles. Take some time to select your text and experiment with the formatting functions. Change the color and size of your text, the background of the page, and add text to the page.

5. Adding Images to Your Page

Adding images to a Web page is very similar to adding an image to a PowerPoint presentation. You can click Insert Item on the menu toolbar and then choose Image. You get the same result when you click the small icon on the formatting bar that looks like a tiny mountain with a sunny sky in the background. The Image dialog box will appear.

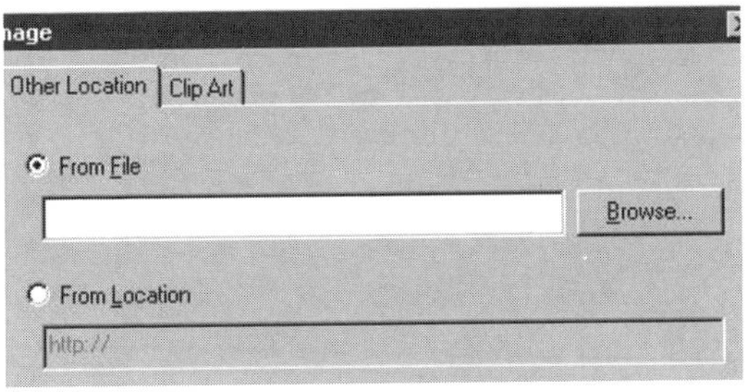

Figure 8g

FrontPage Express does not come with clip art and you will not actually place an image on your page at this point. In order to insert a picture on your Web page, you will need to have a picture or photo available on your hard drive (usually "C") or on a floppy disc (drive "A"). When you click Browse in the image dialog box, you can find your picture by choosing the drive and file name of your image. When you are ready to do more work with Web pages, visit the companion Web site *(www.newtools-online)* for links to FrontPage Express tutorials. These will lead you through some of the more advanced functions of FrontPage Express. For now, leave your FrontPage Express program open as I talk about saving your pages and publishing the Web site.

PUBLISHING YOUR WEB SITE

When it comes time to publish your Web site, you will have to send the files from your computer to a server, which, in turn, shows the pages to the public. In order to do this, you will need to save your pages on your computer. The first task is to save the initial page you have just created. This will become your homepage—the first page people see when they visit your Web site. Go to the menu item File at the top of the screen, then click Save As. The following dialog box will appear:

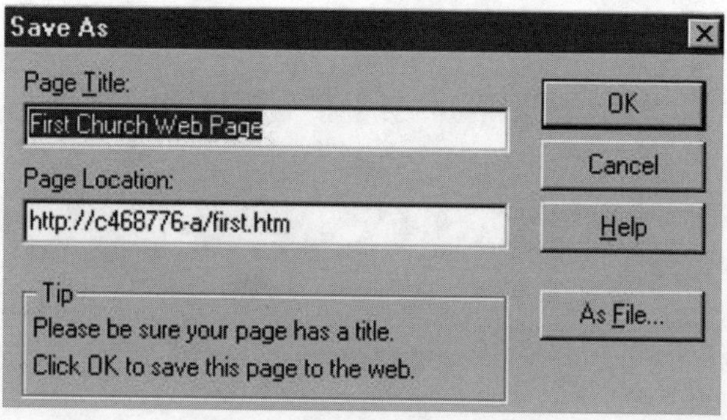

Figure 8h

The default setting for the Save As dialog box will save the file to a Web location. (*Note:* Please be sure your page has a title.) Click OK to save this page to the Web. However, you are going to bypass this way of saving the page because you are not going to save to a Web at this point. When the time comes, you will transfer your pages to a server as individual files. For now, choose As File in the dialog box. A new Save as File dialog box will appear.

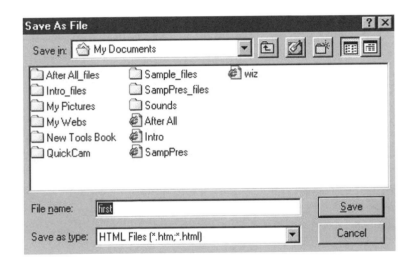

Figure 8i

This step is very important. We want all of our Web pages saved in a convenient, easy-to-find place or "folder" on the computer. For our purposes, we are going to put them on the hard drive ("C" drive) in a folder called "Web Site." Follow these steps carefully:

1. Click the small down arrow just to the right of the window, following Save In. When the submenu appears, choose "C." A new window appears that shows all the folders you have on drive "C." You want to create a new folder on drive "C" where you can save your Web pages.

2. Click the icon that looks like a tiny folder with a kind of star

on the upper right corner. This is the third icon from the right. When you click the icon, New Folder will appear in the screen area, highlighted in blue. Now type in the highlighted box "Web Site," and a new folder called "Web Site" will be created.

3. Double-click the new folder "Web Site." You will now be able to save your Web page in this new folder on drive C.

4. Carefully now, place your cursor in the box called File Name and type "index." If there is any other text in the File Name box, highlight it by selecting the text and then type "index." Now press Save and your file "Index" will be saved on drive C in the folder "Web Site."

Why do we do this? The very first page browsers will look for at any site is "index.htm" (or index.html). "Index" will always be the name of your homepage. When someone first comes to your Web site on the Internet, the very first page the browser will look for at your Web address (URL) is the file (or page) "index.htm." (Actually, the extension—the part of the address that comes after the period at the end of *index*—may be "html," or "shtml," or another extension. All of them are Web pages, and "index" is always the name of the first page that comes up.)

Why is this? The browser needs a way to find the entrance to any Web site, and "index" is the standard name for the entrance. (This makes sense, since an "index" is a resource found in the back of some books that tells you where things are located in the book.) The name for your index page used by most people is your "homepage." You should plan from the very beginning to have a well-organized, easy-to-follow homepage. Once you start surfing the Internet, you will find Web sites where it is easy to get lost. When that happens, it is not because you don't know what you are doing, but because the site is not well organized or easy to navigate.

The next step in publishing a Web site is to send the Web pages to a server for all the world to see. Most ISPs offer free Web space to their customers. Your task will be to transfer the files from your computer to your ISP's server. This is most easily accomplished by a program called an FTP program. FTP stands for "file transfer protocol." It is not mysterious at all, but is simply a program that helps one computer talk to another computer and allows files to be transferred back and forth according to a protocol both can understand. You will hear people use FTP as a verb, as in, "We need to FTP our files to the server." When the time comes, an FTP program will not be so difficult to learn.[3]

Once you have begun to understand the basics of authoring a Web site, it will be important to address some of the planning and administrative tasks that are a part of launching a Web-based ministry.

Chapter Nine

Internet-Based Ministry: Planning

Getting Started

Imagine driving into one of those towns where churches post their signs on the outskirts of the village limits. You've seen them, right? Suppose you were looking for a church to visit this coming weekend and you were going to pick one based on the signs. One sign is bright red with flashing lights and glowing symbols all over it. A neon sign blinks off and on with the words "We've got the best worship!" Another sign looks like it was once a really great sign, but it is so weatherworn you can't read the worship times, and the paint is peeling badly. They obviously have not attended to this sign for some time. The third sign is a simple sign with easy to read lettering for the address, phone number, and worship times. It is colorful but tasteful and could well have been erected this week.

WHERE WOULD YOU ATTEND?

Clearly, if the only impression your church will give a potential visitor is coming from a sign at the outskirts of town, a congregation would be well advised to give some time and attention to how the sign will represent it. Would you, for instance, want to take any of the following approaches to obtaining a presence for your church?

- Joe says he knows how to make signs; let's have him put one out there for us.
- The young people are good at making things. They could do a sign.
- Why don't we buy the pastor some tools and materials and let her do it?

This method of planning could be a disaster. Joe, it turns out, doesn't make such good signs after all. Subsequently, a subcommittee has to be appointed to think up a good way to get rid of Joe's sign without losing Joe and his family as members. Not only does Joe not possess a gift for sign making, he is a very sensitive person to boot.

The youth group, on the other hand, has this kid who is a wizard at electronics. Maybe he could come up with a sign. When he completes the project, the church's new sign at the edge of town is a wonder of adolescent creativity. When a car approaches, a motion detector causes the sign to flash the message "Honk if you love hard rock!" When a car horn sounds, the sign plays the heavy-metal band Metallica's "Nothing Else Matters."

Finally, there is the plight of the pastor. Having gotten her hands on some tools and having begun to do some woodworking for the sign project, she discovers a real gift and now spends twenty-five hours a week on her "woodworking ministry."

"Hmm," the chairperson of the church council says at the next council meeting. "There's more to this sign business than we had thought." Hold on to the sign analogy; it will come in handy as you begin the planning process for your church's Web presence.

Planning

It is difficult to overstate the importance of planning in the development of Internet ministry. A Web site is not necessarily a ministry any more than a building is necessarily a church. Even if a Web site reads "Web Site of First Church," it *still* is not necessarily a ministry any more than a building with a sign out front that reads "First Church" is necessarily a church. I recall seeing a beautiful little white church building out in the country. It had a steeple and a fresh coat of white paint, but the sign out front read "Anderson's Antique Mall." There is an old saying used by real estate salespersons that states the three most important factors in real estate are "location, location, location." It can equally be affirmed that the three most important factors in Web ministry are "planning, planning, planning." There are thousands upon thousands of church Web sites, but only a small percentage of them can honestly be called Web ministries.

A local church needs to consider three essential questions before considering a Web presence. These questions will take you through a process that leads naturally from the initial consideration of a Web site to the published product. If you do not go through the process carefully, not only will your Web presence *not* help the work of your congregation, it could hinder it.

Why? Who? How?

Be prepared to ask the question "Why?" the first time the issue of producing a Web site for the church is raised. Someone says to the pastor, "Wouldn't it be great if we had a Web site?" Or a member of the Christian education committee, whose husband builds computers, says, "What this church needs is a Web site." Whether it is a Web site, or a sign at the edge of town, the first question that needs to be raised is, Why do we want a Web site?

Some reasons for creating a Web site are not so good. Reasons like "First Church has one; we're going to fall behind if we don't get one" or, "If we don't have a Web site, we're behind the times." And then there's the old evangelism hook: "A Web site will draw visitors to our church." Motivation like this will set your church's technology plan on autopilot headed for a crash.

There are, however, some very good reasons to have a Web presence for your church. It can serve a growing Internet-user population in the same way the Yellow Pages serves a telephone-user population. That is, a Web presence offers one more way to publicize your ministry. Your membership or evangelism committee will have an interest in outreach possibilities using the Internet. A Web presence can offer a means of communicating with church members as well as a way for members to communicate with one another. The youth and Christian education departments may have input for ways they would like to use an Internet presence. Many congregations have used the Internet as a way to reach out to the community with information and resources for particular social issues.

It will soon become clear that the task of designing, creating, and maintaining an Internet presence will need to involve more than one person. At this point the question "Who?" will become increasingly important. Churches that have a successful, enduring Internet ministry enjoy the encouragement and support of the staff and governing board and the volunteer efforts of a group. As you begin the process, gather a Web ministry task group to do some initial data gathering. This group should bring its results to the governing board and staff along with recommendations for the church's Web ministry. Even in the smallest churches, it is important to involve as many people as possible in planning and implementing a Web ministry. Set a goal of having your Internet ministry on par with any other church ministry. In this way, it will become a vital, functioning part of the church's life.

As the planning gets under way, you should have copies of "Planning Your Web Presence," which is included in the Appendix. (It can be printed out from the companion Web site.) Gather your planning group and work through this exercise. The first sheet helps you look at the issue of why you would build a Web site. As part of this analysis it will be helpful to make some important visits. First of all, you should visit other churches' Web sites. Just as church members will frequently visit other churches when a building program is developed, so visiting other churches on the Web will help you gain a clearer picture of what is good and what is not good in church Web design. The second visit you should make is to each area of your church's ministry. Even in small congregations, there are several areas of worship, education, and fellowship that should be considered in the development of a Web site. It will soon become very clear that there is much more that *could* be done with a Web site than you can actually accomplish when you first begin. Just as sometimes a building program in a local church will include two or three phases—a Christian education building serves as the worship space until a completed sanctuary is added—so also a Web site may develop in two or more phases. You may be sure that planning ahead of time will save headaches in the future.

As you work through the "Why?" questions of your Web site, brainstorm about ways the Internet presence can become a ministry where your site has its own niche. What, for example, could your site do that would draw visitors and provide something that no one else does? You might decide to provide an extensive collection of information and resources for elder care in your county. You could list the nursing homes, day care programs, government assistance options, names of directors and social workers in elder care facilities, and support groups for families who are struggling with Alzheimer's disease. You could plan a phase-two development of your Web site that would provide interactive discussion boards for families. When people come to appreciate your Web ministry and visit often, you have the opportunity to gently nudge them toward your fellowship.

When you have worked through the "whys" of your Web ministry, you should conclude by writing out a clear mission statement for the Web ministry. Using the term *Web ministry* instead of just *Web site* will keep the focus on your church's Web presence as more than just sticking a page out in cyberspace. This fact cannot be overstated: Until you are ready to deploy a Web ministry, it is best to refrain from posting a Web page.

Here's something that may be difficult to believe when you are just beginning to look into Web ministry, but it has proved true: It is easier to develop your skills in creating an Internet presence than it is to develop a team to do the required planning that will result in an authentic Web ministry. "Less is more" applies to the majority of church Web sites.

One of the cardinal rules in preparing a Web site for your ministry is to resist the temptation to rush to publication. Planning for the content and securing the commitment of people to work with this ministry are more critical than learning how to write Web pages and send them to a server. If you think of a Web site as a kind of curriculum, you know that it is much easier to come by good curriculum than it is to find the people to implement and teach the curriculum.

After preparing the mission statement, the second major planning task is to raise the "Who?" questions of creating a Web ministry. "Who?" questions will help you determine if the broad scope of your initial planning is too much or too little. If there is only one person who will learn to write Web pages, do all of the maintenance, and update the site, then you will need to narrow the scope of what you expect to do. This step will also help your group make some decisions about a timeline for your project and reflect on the work that needs to be done with the congregation before you actually deploy a Web site. You want to recruit volunteers and gather resources for training as a beginning step and then move toward developing your Web ministry. You should have a minimum of two persons who can write, maintain, and deploy the church's Web pages. It is too easy for one person to move away, become ill, lose interest, or otherwise give up the task. Additionally, when at least two people are working at a task, mutual encouragement will bring better results in a shorter period of time. Jesus had a reason for sending his disciples out for their first mission trip in pairs: It doubled the chances of success.

The third major area for planning raises the "How?" questions of Web ministry. These questions will help your group come to terms with the nuts and bolts of Web site production and publication. This is the point at which you will want to involve people who have some knowledge of Web site production and publishing or who are willing to accept the task of learning the basics.

When you discuss how to go about creating and publishing a Web site, be sure to review the issues that have already been discussed in this chapter. It is a good idea to go over the issues again with your planning tools in hand. Do you want to develop a more extensive site or simply post a kind of church brochure? Do you want to use a free service to host your page, or do you intend to design and author your own pages? The planning sheets will help you to move the process along.

There is one step I recommend to every church that is considering developing a Web ministry: Secure your own domain name!

Getting your own domain name is simple and inexpensive. You can get a domain name and hold it even if you are not ready to publish your site. The cost can be as low as $36 for two years. Obtaining a domain name is simple. There are several organizations that can help with securing and registering a domain name. One good place to start is *www.buydomains.com*. This Web site allows you to search for a domain name and then register the name. It will also hold the name for you until you are ready to publish. Here's an important tip. *Any* ISP can host your domain. Ask your ISP about hosting yours. When you own your own domain, the term used for your domain is *virtual*. When you own a domain name, it is called a "virtual domain." Ask the ISPs you talk with what they charge to host a virtual domain.[1] Once you secure the name you want, there is no need to rush into publication. Patience in preplanning your site will pay off when the time comes for publication.

A domain name is the part of an Internet address (URL) that comes between the "www." and ".com." It is a primary Web site address. In other words, the URL for a domain is a top-level name. When you publish your church's Web site on your ISP's server as a Web site under the ISP's domain, your URL will include the ISP's name followed by your name. An example would be a Web site that is located at an ISP called genevaonline. Genevaonline's domain name is *www.genevaonline.com*. If I were to publish a church Web site on Genevaonline's server, it would have a URL of something like: *www.genevaonline.com/~firstchurch*. Churches that include the possibility of Web ministry should obtain a domain name as the first step in gaining an identity for their Internet presence.

The domain name of this book's companion Web site is, for instance, newtools-online. When you put the name after "www." and before ".com," you have a domain name: *www.newtools-online.com*. The name is easy to remember and provides an identity for the site. The last part of the URL is the extension. The most common extensions are ".com," used by businesses; ".net," also used by businesses and other organizations; and ".org," used mainly by nonprofit organizations. Most churches use the extension ".org." Some churches that really want their names will use ".com" or ".net" if the

".org" version is taken. For instance, the following three domain names are all taken:

www.firstmethodist.com
www.firstmethodist.net
www.firstmethodist.org

Chances are you will find that the names of almost any denominational church are already taken. Substitute "Presbyterian," "Congregational," or any other denominational name and you will more than likely find a local church Web site. You can have a bit of fun while exploring local church Web sites by typing in various church names. Try *www.stjohnsepiscopal.com,* or *www.stjohnsepiscopal.net,* or *www.stjohnsepiscopal.org* and you will find a Web site.

Work with your planning team to find a domain name for your church. Most denomination names like First Methodist, Westminster Presbyterian, St. John's Episcopal, and First Congregational are taken. You might combine a town name along with your church name or merge a location name with your church name in order to find a domain name that is not taken. When you choose a name, the name will be all lowercase letters or a combination of letters and numbers with no spaces. If you are a First Methodist church in some town or city, you could try for the name *www.1methodist.org.* (Yup. It's taken!) In other words, creativity will help when choosing a name. As a bonus, you will have some fun in the process and get to visit all kinds of church Web sites. (Most will provide examples of how *not* to build a local church Web site.)

Chapter Ten

Christian Education and Youth Ministry

Equipping the Church School of the Twenty-first Century

Technology has changed the educational landscape dramatically in the past few years. Even so, we are still just beginning to see how this technology will be integrated into our schools and affect our children's learning. One of the top priorities of the U.S. Department of Education is to provide educational opportunities aimed toward computer literacy and Internet access for all schoolchildren. The department's Web site included the following from a call to action in which corporate partners were being sought to assist with the priority:

For children to succeed, they need to master basic skills at an early age. A critical element of this is the need for information and technological literacy. To help achieve these aims, we must focus on a comprehensive approach to integrating technology into teaching and learning while recognizing that—as powerful as technology is—it is no substitute for an inspiring teacher or a loving parent. Together, we must:

1. Connect every classroom to the Internet
2. Ensure that all students have modern multi-media computer access, ideally at a ratio of 1 computer for every 4-5 students

3. Ensure that teachers are technologically literate and can integrate technology into the curriculum

4. Make available high quality educational software and online learning resources[1]

The continuing development of computer literacy and the push for access to information technology will shape our educational agenda for the foreseeable future. As this trend shapes our children's educational experience, it will also have an effect on their *Christian* educational experience. Our children will experience learning in an interactive, self-directed way that compels interest and enthusiasm. Computer-mediated learning provides the kind of hands-on, experiential learning that helps build skills and increase knowledge.

It is significant to note that the Department of Education's call to action includes the recognition that "as powerful as technology is— it is no substitute for an inspiring teacher or a loving parent." This is exactly the kind of perspective we want to bring to the use of technology in the church. Technology is powerful and it can harness all the benefits for the church that the schools will experience, but it is not a substitute for an inspiring Christian teacher or a loving Christian community.

Technology, as noted earlier, should be a servant and not the master of our educational enterprise. The use of new technological tools with our educational programs in the church will not mean the end of difficulties for Sunday schools and youth ministries. Declining enrollment and attendance in the church's educational programs will not be automatically reversed by a sudden introduction of computers and digital equipment into the system. The development of an administrative plan for educational ministry must consist of more than simply adding computers and Internet access to the Sunday school. Here are a few steps that will increase the opportunities for success in planning for technology implementation in Christian education and youth ministry.

1. Devote the same time and energy planning for the introduction of technology into education and youth ministries as you would for your Web ministry. Modify the planning sheets used

     in the section on Web ministry and use them for educational ministry.

2. A critical analysis of the current educational and youth ministries of your church should take place along with technology planning. Books like Charles R. Foster's *Educating Congregations: The Future of Christian Education* (Nashville: Abingdon Press) can be helpful in completing an evaluation of the church's current situation. Using Foster's analysis and exercises along with technology planning could bring exciting results to your educational ministry.

3. Following the suggestions in chapter 6, do an analysis of what is available in your current inventory of audiovisual equipment.

4. Start smart! Begin with a few small steps in bringing new approaches to teaching and learning in the Sunday school and youth programs in light of your current situation. Success in one small project will create more goodwill for your program than a proposal for a complete overhaul of your current system. People who are not familiar with some of the new possibilities that technology can bring to your program are frequently overwhelmed by information overload.

Careful analysis and planning will help you avoid the pitfalls that come with introducing new technologies. A major mistake many groups make when implementing technology is to purchase equipment prior to analyzing churchwide needs. A second critical error is adopting plans without including the people who have primary interest in the program. I know of one instance where a new computer was purchased for a youth group. It turns out the group was very interested in producing digital video, but the computer did not have enough RAM to process video.

Student-Centered Teaching

It is very important for teachers to develop skills in student-centered teaching so that young people will be interested in learning new technologies. Think for a moment about the differences between Sunday school as our oldest members remember it and Sunday school today.

A discussion between a Sunday school superintendent and the church's first- and second-grade Sunday school teacher demonstrates two differing approaches to education. The superintendent had grown up in the church and could remember a time when almost one hundred children crowded the small building. The teacher was a newer member of the church, a mother of two elementary-age boys, who, until recently, had not been active in a church since her school days. "We could really use more space," the teacher said. "I usually have about seven energetic children in my class and I would like to set up some learning centers."

"My goodness," the superintendent replied. "We used to have thirty children in this classroom! They would come and sit quietly for an hour while I taught the lesson." (The class enrollment then was thirty-five.)

The superintendent was a product of a *content*-centered Christian education. And it worked for her and her friends. She and her generation attended Sunday school regularly, where they were expected to sit quietly and listen to the teacher. Disrupting the class was not tolerated, and parents—who were attending their own classes—expected their children to behave in Sunday school. Thirty of the thirty-five class members attended regularly. The superintendent remembers when she was a child in this same Sunday school. She and her friends had fun, sang songs, learned the Bible, and felt as though the church was their Sunday morning home.

The central focus of the Christian educational process was the content learned. At the end of the third-grade Sunday school class, most of the children could recite the Ten Commandments, the books of the Old and New Testaments, and the Beatitudes.

On the other hand, the young mother who is a teacher is a product of a different generation. Parents of the children in her class attend church sporadically and many do not attend worship at all. Although there are nineteen children enrolled in her class, the average attendance is seven. The *content*-centered approach to teaching does not work because so many children are absent for many of the lessons. The parents do not participate in any church-sponsored educational events and are not well versed in the content of the faith. For those few parents who do encourage attendance, family structure often complicates regular attendance. Some children spend every other weekend with a mom or dad who is now married to a stepparent.

The superintendent and the teacher are equally concerned about the Christian education of their church's children. One is not right and the other wrong. Each person is simply a product of her culture.

An example of the cultural differences between these two women came about when the congregation voted to remodel the Sunday school area and fellowship hall. Everyone agreed that updating was necessary. The disagreement occurred when the issue of financing was raised. The demographics of the church were such that the congregation was almost evenly divided between a senior population and young families in their late twenties to early forties. One proposal involved asking for pledges to pay for the $60,000 project and to begin work when the funds were in hand. The other approach included taking out a mortgage for the amount and to begin the remodeling immediately. A vote was evenly divided. Can you imagine which group voted for the cash-in-hand approach and which wanted to secure the mortgage? One of the older members of the church spoke at the meeting and made a very revealing comment. "My parents lived through the depression," he said. "We lost our home when the bank foreclosed, and from that day on my father warned us against taking on debt." After the meeting, a young father noted, "I remember my grandfather talking like that. It was a whole other world, wasn't it?"

One of the ways to close this generation gap would be to have every member of your planning team under the age of sixty read Tom Brokaw's book *The Greatest Generation* (New York: Random House, 1998), which I mentioned earlier. There has never been a time in church history when the differences between the childhood lives of the oldest and youngest members have been more radical.

The superintendent and the teacher have worldviews that are as different as those of the Jew and the Greek in Paul's time. Paul was concerned only to bring the gospel to people whose worldview and culture were dramatically different from that of his Jewish brothers and sisters. He wrote, "I have become all things to all people, that I might by all means save some. I do it all for the sake of the gospel, so that I may share in its blessings" (1 Corinthians 9:22*b*-23).

Student-centered teaching in the church does not mean that content is unimportant, but that the context of ministry has changed. Children and teenagers today live in a culture that is radically different from the culture their counterparts experienced three to five decades ago. Student-centered teaching requires that we work with children and young people using tools that are familiar to them. These tools can help them engage the content of the faith and hold their interest while providing an opportunity to pass on values and content that can change their lives. Most children are eager learners when given the opportunity to use their natural creativity and inquisitive natures. A Sunday school teacher who understands student-centered learning becomes a guide or a coach. The teacher guides a group in learning adventures. She or he is someone who coaches a group of young learners and models the joy of exploratory learning. The teacher who successfully reaches out to children and teenagers in our culture is someone who takes the time to learn the tools they are familiar with, engages students in mutual learning, and provides new avenues for exploring the good news.

Building Community Through Collaborative Learning

There is a model of exploring, learning, and community building that can be instructive for our work with young people in the church today. Although on the surface the model may seem unlikely, it is a NASA space shuttle mission. Each launch of a space shuttle includes a crew of six to eight persons. The crew becomes a team that learns and works together for an extended period of time in preparation for a mission. The shuttle crew becomes a self-contained team of persons who are dependent upon one another for successful completion of their mission. The crew includes pilots and specialists in several scientific disciplines. A successful mission requires the skills and cooperation of every single member of the crew. There is no such thing as a crew member without a function. Each NASA space shuttle mission is an amazing illustration of collaborative planning, learning, and action. When there is success—and there usually is—all members of the crew share in the joy of a mission accomplished. Even when a mission encounters difficulty, as did the second flight of the space shuttle *Columbia,* the community is drawn together to share in the tough times and celebrate what was good. In spite of the fact that the mission was delayed and then cut almost three days short, 90 percent of the mission objectives were met and new discoveries were made.[2]

The biblical model for this cohesive, community-oriented group life is the Body of Christ. In an individualistic "I did it my way" culture, the NASA mission may speak more clearly to our youth culture.

The NASA model could translate directly to our work with children and teens in the church. A class or a group can become engaged in a mission of exploration and learning in which all members have a function and a direct impact on the outcome. For example, a class or group accepts a mission to bring members who are homebound or in nursing homes to worship. Because it is not physically possible to do this, the group decides to make a visit to each of the shut-ins, take a photograph, and make an audio recording of each homebound member. A member of the group (the crew) has access to a digital camera; another knows how to bring the photographs into a PowerPoint presentation. Still another crew member is able to take the audiotapes and produce sound files for the computer that can also be brought into the PowerPoint presentation. The crew then produces a program in which the shut-in members of the church can be seen and heard.

The project turns out so well that the pastor decides to use the presentation at prayer time during worship. The entire congregation has the opportunity to reconnect with people who have not been present with them in worship for some time. When the mission crew members witness the power of this presentation to move the congregation, they will become more connected themselves and will be inspired to develop future missions.[3]

The important components of collaborative learning are (1) a clear, well-planned mission, (2) a willing crew where each member has a specific function, (3) tools to complete the mission, and (4) a clear outcome, where results of the mission have a direct effect on the community.

A collaborative model of teaching and learning creates opportunities for working with children and teens in the church outside of the traditional appeals for Sunday school teachers. The superintendent I spoke of earlier has a perpetual struggle with finding enough Sunday school teachers. She rarely, however, has difficulty in recruiting moms or grandmothers to help with making the children's costumes for the Christmas pageant or dads and grandfathers to construct a manger. The use of new technologies in the educational and youth ministries of the church will provide increasing opportunities for all members to use their skills in the task of collaborative learning and community building.

Engaging the Youth Group in Learning and Mission

Traditional methods of engaging children and young people in the educational ministry of the church relied on gathering curriculum (the content), announcing class times, and asking parents to bring their children to class at the appropriate time. There was nothing wrong with the content of the program. The aim of the curriculum was to teach the life and times of Jesus. Our superintendent's generation did very well with this. Children were brought to class by parents who then attended their own class. The church learned.

This same process of announcing class times and lesson plans will have an entirely different result for the young mom who is teaching seven children. She hopes to engage her children by having opportunities for them to use their creativity in a hands-on way. In other words, it is not the *content* of the plan that is missing the mark, it is the *context* that works against the goal of engaging children in learning about the life of Christ.

When faced with a generation that is not present for the teaching and whose parents may not be motivated to gain the learning we are called to bring to them, it is time to reexamine the methods we are using. The key to engaging our children and youth in learning and mission is to go back to basics ourselves and look once again at the methods Jesus used. The fact is that Jesus sent his disciples into a world where the challenge was more similar to the challenge we face today than it was to the challenge faced by our dear, committed superintendent.

When Jesus gave his final instructions to his disciples he did not say, "Open your doors and invite all nations to come and be baptized. Then teach those people everything I have taught you." You do recall the way he said it, right? The operative term was "Go!"

If the children are not in church these days then we must "go!" If our teenagers have not been in church lately then we must "go!" And if the parents of these children and teenagers have not been in church during the past few years then we must "go!"

When we "go!" we will need to understand the culture we are going to and learn to speak the language the culture speaks. Our vocabulary will have to include things like "ISP," "digital files," and "CD-RW." Engaging our children does not require a brand-new thing at all, but recovering an ancient way: recalling a time when the disciples were *sent* and the church obediently *went*. Perhaps the difficulty in reaching the culture is actually an opportunity to do what has always brought new life to a struggling church. Namely, moving out of the comfortable confines of the church into the challenging culture of the world.

There are some encouraging clues to how we should handle the task we face. Children and teenagers have some very clear interests we can tap into. They take quickly to the new technologies and love some of the things they can do. They love music, video, and are generally computer literate. They love to talk to one another and will spend lots of time talking on the phone, chatting in a chat room, and searching for information on the Internet. They are very much attached to their peers and enjoy trying new things.

Do you see? They are a field "ripe unto harvest" for a church that is willing to invest itself in the tools and technologies they are familiar with and willing to learn and grow with them. Chapter 13 will explore some ideas you can use in your local church. Many of them can be used in Christian education and youth ministry.

For now, here is one surefire idea you could use to gather a crew of young people for a mission that could energize the whole church. Commission your youth leaders to talk to or call every single young person in the church and challenge them with something like this:

> Jennifer, this is Mr. Jewell, the youth director at church. I am trying to get a group of our young people and their friends to help write and produce a movie on poverty in our county. We are going to use the movie in church and maybe take it to a local television station. Would you be willing to get together with me and a few of the kids to talk about doing this?[4]

Successfully engaging young people in learning and mission today will require some new ways of delivering "the faith that was once for all entrusted to the saints" (Jude 3). Nevertheless, the task may be more within our reach today than it has been for some time if we can make the connection between the *content* of our faith and the *culture* of our young people. The tools are available; we need only the time and the talent of those in the church who care.

Chapter Eleven

Media Arts
in Worship

Our Visual Culture

A revolution in media was on the horizon as the twentieth century dawned. In December 1895, Auguste and Louis Lumière gave the first commercial demonstration of a film projector. The world had no idea what loomed ahead as filmmakers were experimenting with various methods of producing the motion picture. Auguste Lumière said of the projector, "Our invention can be exploited for a certain time as a scientific curiosity, but apart from that, it has no commercial future whatsoever."[1] By 1927 the movie industry had transitioned from the nickelodeon and short films to feature-length silent movies.[2]

There is a strong parallel between the beginning of the movie industry and the beginning of the digital revolution that began with the personal computer. Both have undergone amazing changes from their beginnings. No one could have predicted the impact each would have on the culture. And no serious scholar could have conceived of the idea that print media would ever be dominated by visual media.

The film industry took a giant leap forward with the advent of talking films. The year 1939 signaled a harbinger of things to come when films like *Gone with the Wind* and *The Wizard of Oz* took the nation by storm. Hollywood became the international center for visual arts.

One would never have predicted that there would be anything else similar to Hollywood's impact on visual media. But in retrospect, it is easy to see how the advent of television in the mid-twentieth century helped complete a transition from print-dominated media to visual media. There was a hint of this transition when some of us older church members went to the theater to "see" the news. Do you remember the short newsreels that were shown in movie theaters before the feature film? The newsreels gave us visual news, radio supplied news we could hear, and newspapers were the primary source of detailed information about national and world events. News traveled much more slowly and we listened to it or read it. Radio and reading supplied much of the entertainment for many of our older church members in their earliest years. The advent of television made it possible for every home to have access to visual media.

The baby boomer generation, defined by some as those people who were born between 1946 and 1964, has experienced a revolution in media and the near-complete transition from print to visual media. Television is quickly being replaced by the personal computer as the primary instrument of information technology. The window to the world for most homes is no longer the family television. It is now the family computer. And with this window, the information flow is no longer one way. Information does not just flow in, but also flows out. Late-breaking news with accompanying video is available on demand. Children and grandchildren of the boomers are completely captivated by visual media. It is not enough to hear their favorite musician, they want to see the artist. Music videos have become a multimillion-dollar business in the new economy.

The influence of our visual culture on the church has been progressive. From filmstrip to 16mm film projectors to videotape, we have steadily invested in visual media. Recent advances in visual technologies and the increasing availability of broadband Internet access will accelerate this impact. The brief historical view of the maturation of visual media should alert us to a key issue. Those of us who are in leadership positions in the church have grown up as the visual media we are familiar with has also grown up. The generation of young people in our churches that will soon become the leadership of the twenty-first-century church is growing up with digital media. They do not have to transition to new forms of media; they have never lived without them. If the use of digital video media in the context of worship is a struggle for many of us, it will be natural for them.

This brings us to the fact that one of the areas of church life that can benefit greatly from the dramatic growth of visual technologies is worship. Any discussion of using visual technologies in worship needs to take into account the fact that visual aids have been a part of worship for centuries. The church has used art forms like stained-glass windows, ornate statuary, stations of the cross, and Warner Sallman's Head of Christ to teach and to inspire. The advent of computer-aided graphic production and the LCD projector brings new ways to use media-assisted visual arts in worship. It is important to be aware that this area, more than any other in our exploration of technologies in ministry, will be a sensitive one. Many of us have experienced worship wars, where worship styles have been at the heart of no little controversy. The field of worship can also be a field of land mines! These land mines, however, are not so simple to deal with. An easy answer would be to simply avoid the field, but it is not just making changes that can be troublesome. It is frequently not making changes that can bring trouble. The American landscape is littered with tiny churches where folks gather with the confidence that they have won out with their "We never did it that way before" liturgy.

The question is: What is the best way to worship? The answer is: The best way to worship is the way that brings us into the presence of our awesome God. The practical implication of this for worship in the twenty-first-century church is that we move ahead with all deliberate caution and sensitivity in applying the wealth of digital technologies in our life together, including our worship life.

No Longer Lonely: Creating a Worship-Planning Team

Worship planning in the majority of local churches has been primarily the pastor's function. When the pastor is the solo clergy staff person in a church, he or she has the complete responsibility for planning and conducting worship. When the church is busy or the pastor's life is particularly rushed, the worship-planning function can get shortchanged. Even more planning is required during those times when special services are conducted, a dramatic reading is used, or when laypersons are becoming more involved in worship. When a church begins to consider using media arts in worship, a planning team is absolutely essential to success. This is one of the secondary benefits of using technology to assist worship. The pastor is no longer alone in planning and conducting worship when these new aids are used. This is mostly good for worship because a lack of planning for worship is essentially a guarantee for uninspired worship.

Success in introducing and implementing media-assisted visual arts in worship requires careful and sensitive forethought. There are several steps to consider as you develop this ministry.

STAGE ONE: THE PLANNING TEAM

Gather a Stage One planning team of four to seven persons. The team should include:

- Someone with technological knowledge and skill
- A person who has been involved in and has an understanding of worship
- Someone who has a fair degree of biblical literacy and cares for the educational ministry of the church
- Representatives from the generations that are present in your church (this representation could include people who are already on the team)
- The pastor or pastors

Stage One planning is a broad-based overview of how various forms of media might be used in worship. Team members should read this book, or at least read part 2 of the book, in which I examine the essentials of and leadership in using technology in ministry.

The first step the team will take is to do a careful analysis of the current worship life of the congregation. Have the team members complete the following exercise separately and then do the exercise as a group. Then spend time discussing your church's readiness for introducing media arts in worship.[3]

1. Our Current Worship Style
   - ☐ Very Liturgical—few if any changes each week
   - ☐ Somewhat liturgical—follows a liturgical pattern, but some changes
   - ☐ Structured, but not committed to one style
   - ☐ Not very structured, with frequent changes

2. Current Use of Media (film, slides, overhead projection images)
   - ☐ Never
   - ☐ Occasional—once or twice a year
   - ☐ Once a quarter or more
   - ☐ Frequently—at least once a month

3. Size of our congregation in average adult worship attendance
   - ☐ Over 500
   - ☐ 250–499
   - ☐ 100–249
   - ☐ 99 or fewer

4. Demographics of Our Congregation
   - ☐ Average age over 62
   - ☐ Average age 50–61
   - ☐ Equal numbers of younger and older adult members
   - ☐ Average age 45 and under

When you have completed this short exercise, give points to your answers. The first item in each category is worth 4 points, the second 3 points, the third 2 points, and the fourth 1 point. For instance, if you checked the first item in each category, you have a score of 16 points. If your team has a consensus that your congregation scores 16 points, then you would likely do well to introduce LCD projection anywhere in the church except the sanctuary. This does not mean that there can never be any successful use of new technologies in worship, it simply means using a cautious approach, which I will discuss in the next section. A score of 4 points, on the other hand, would signal a readiness and enthusiasm for using computer-assisted media in worship.

The following breakdown will give you a sense for your church's "RQ" (Readiness Quotient):

4–6 Points	Low Resistance
7–9 Points	Some Resistance
10–13 Points	Moderate Resistance
14–16 Points	High Resistance

Caution: This is not a definitive guide, but a beginning place to discuss your congregation's readiness for introducing media in worship. There are exceptions to every rule. Youth does not necessarily guarantee enthusiasm for change, and age does not necessarily translate to resistance.

STAGE TWO: INTRODUCING MEDIA IN WORSHIP

This is the point at which a Stage Two planning team will begin developing specific ideas for implementation. The composition of this group could include persons from the Stage One group, but should include persons who will work with longer-term development of media for worship. At least two should have knowledge of or a willingness to learn PowerPoint (or other presentation software) and use of the personal computer and LCD projector.

Stage Two should begin by considering what opportunities may be available for introducing media in worship.

• In cases where you currently have a single Sunday morning service, are there enough people to warrant adding a second service?

- If the congregation's size does not permit more than one service, would the gradual introduction of media, in portions of the service, give our program a better chance of success?
- Would it make more sense to institute a Saturday evening media service? Are there enough people to support a service like this?
- If the church is of the liturgical tradition, the addition of a service of the Word or a special service of the daily office could be a possibility.

Only you and your team can design something that will work for your congregation. A series of questions and statements like those above will help in developing your congregation's profile and suggest the best way to proceed. By putting together the possibilities for introducing media in worship with your church's "RQ," you will have insight into how to proceed.

Here are three possibilities for how teams in different congregations might go about their task. The assumption is that these congregations have one Sunday morning service with just under one hundred people in attendance. The worship planning team in each church agrees that a second service is not a feasible alternative.

1. The planning team at First Church expects that resistance to introducing media in worship will be high, so they decide to show a PowerPoint presentation during coffee hour of the youth group's mission trip. They will use a laptop computer hooked up to an LCD projector and the program will be projected onto a screen. The slides will cycle through the program continuously. They will follow this up a few weeks later with a program featuring audio of the Sunday school children singing, accompanied by slides of the various classes. The team plans to introduce the congregation to the newer technologies in a context that will not be threatening. The expectation is that by using subjects and material dear to the members' hearts, namely children and youth, interest in using the new tools will grow. As planning team members patiently develop their programs and listen to the congregation, they work on themes and possibilities for future use in worship.

2. A team at Church of the Savior expects resistance to be some-

where on the moderate to low continuum. They plan to introduce the congregation to using a computer and LCD projector during the worship service by using a PowerPoint presentation during the preservice announcement time. Two weeks before the program, the church will make a short announcement that a special report is being prepared that will show some of the mission work the church is involved in. The program will highlight the need for contributions to the local food pantry. Text and photographs will be used in an animated presentation showing the food pantry staff at work and the families it helps coming for assistance. The three-minute presentation will be accompanied by the hymn "O Master, Let Me Walk with Thee." The team feels it is important to use familiar hymns, scriptures, and images to illustrate that the use of new technologies does not mean the elimination of those things the church has grown to love.

Following the initial program, the team is planning two additional presentations to be used a month apart. The second program will feature presentations on the church's youth and educational ministries, and the third will be "a day in the life of the pastor." Meanwhile, the team will work on presentations that will project the scripture lessons and words to hymns, which will be large enough to help persons who need large-print Bibles and hymnals. From here they will move toward illustrated sermon outlines that will include images of biblical sites and other graphics to help illustrate the day's theme.

3. New Hope Community Church has a planning team that expects very low resistance to introducing computer-aided media in worship. Team members are working with the pastor to introduce using film clips to bring life situations into focus. Advance publicity will inform the congregation of a special sermon on grief. The message will use the funeral scene from *Steel Magnolias*, where a mother is burying her daughter. The daughter is also a young mother who leaves behind a husband and a young child. The highlight of the clip is the mother's reaction to a friend who tells her that the daughter is "in a better place." Her reaction is one that hits home for all persons who have lost someone they love. "I understand that in my head," the mom cries with a mix of grief and anger, "but I wish someone could explain it to my heart!"

The planning team will be working with the pastor to develop film-clip sermon illustrations, PowerPoint presentations that can illustrate current events, and other ways to use media in worship to enhance the message and the ministry of the church.

STAGE THREE: FEEDBACK

A third essential step in the planning team's work is contained in three imperatives: Evaluate. Refine. Evaluate. As your team members continue their work, they are informed by the principle that they are not producing a tech show to dazzle the congregation, but serving the ancient message by enhancing contemporary Christians' ability to engage the good news of Christ.

One of the ways to increase a congregation's acceptance level for using technology in ministry is to provide lots of opportunity for feedback and interaction. A discussion corner at the coffee hour led by a member or members of the planning team can provide immediate reaction to the service. Discussion groups held through the week could offer a way for church members to share their views and suggest their own ideas for developing the media ministry.

The aim of computer-assisted media in worship is not replacing what the church has been used to, but enhancing what is already good. Most people who went from using a typewriter to a computer with a word processing program did not immediately throw out the typewriter. Another point to consider is rehearsal time. While doing the first few programs using the computer, the LCD projector, or other equipment, add up the amount of time it will take you to set up and rehearse the program. Now multiply by 2.5! Nothing will increase a congregation's resistance to using media in worship more than having a five-minute period of dead time while a computer operator plays with wires, muttering, "I just know this should plug into that."

However, you should plan on the fact that someday, somehow, the projector bulb will burn out, the computer will lock up, the wrong DVD clip will show up on-screen, or the power will go out in the middle of a presentation. And someone will say, "See, I told you technology isn't reliable. I liked it the way we used to do it!" Don't argue with him or her. There are two things to remember when the unthinkable finally happens to you:

1. Consider a response to the person who says he doesn't like all this unreliable technology such as, "Yes, you're probably right. And come to think of it, so are human beings unreliable. Someday the pastor might get sick right before worship and there we would be without a sermon." (Hopefully the person will forgive your tongue-in-cheek response.)
2. Be prepared with a "glitch" plan and implement the plan immediately if your program won't work or quits in the middle. If the film clip from *Steel Magnolias* should stop before it is completed, the pastor simply fills in the blanks from the notes she brought with her to the pulpit. If the presentation about the food pantry does not come up, someone from the mission committee immediately stands and gives the report. Remember, you came to the sanctuary, classroom, or fellowship hall early to be sure everything was in order. (Remember my point about rehearsal time!) With proper planning, your glitches will be fewer and your "I told you sos" heard less often.

Some of the ideas in chapter 13 can be used or adapted for use in worship. As you develop a program tailored for your ministry context and work with some of the tools I have discussed, you will surprise yourself with what you can do. There is a whole world of resources "out there" on the Internet and "in there" in the congregation. Most really good ideas for ministry using technological tools have not come from the technology experts at all, but from everyday people who are rooted in the church and who venture into technology use to assist what they already know. Some of the finest presentations and most inspiring work I have seen have come from my students. They already had the inspiration within, and the technology they learned was simply a new and powerful way for them to express it.

Part Four

HOW TO GET THERE FROM HERE

The material in this introductory volume covers a significant number of areas: from beginning computer terminology to selection of equipment to applying new technological tools in ministry. It is not possible to do it all in one volume; there is much more to talk about at another time. For now, it is time to look at administrative issues in moving toward technology use in ministry and finally explore a few ideas for further work.

Chapter Twelve

Three Central Components: People, Program, and Pieces

As you begin the work of introducing new technological tools to the ministry of your church, it is important to keep three central components of your plan in perspective. The order of these components is absolutely intentional. The most important factor in all of your work is the people or personnel, second comes program, and the last piece of the puzzle is "pieces." ("Pieces" being the computers, projectors, software, and the skills to use these tools.) When you first consider the task of learning to use new equipment and acquiring the skills to make the equipment work, you may feel a bit intimidated. However, you will soon discover that the skills will come easily enough. It will quickly become apparent that people issues are priority number one.

People

- The first need of any program is to find the people who will use the equipment you purchase. The commitment of these folks to your aims and goals will be essential.
- People will assess what you do and greet your work with enthusiasm or resistance, so every moment spent easing their transition to new forms of ministry will pay off in increased success. No one I know of has successfully jammed technology

down the throats of people in a *voluntary* organization. (If you are giving people a healthy paycheck to learn this business you *might* force it on them, but even this is becoming more questionable.)

- People are the vehicles God uses to build the church. Gifts for ministry are given to *people,* not programs or pieces of equipment.
- Keeping all the people who are involved in or affected by this new ministry at the top of the priority list will keep the focus on ministry.

Some years ago, a church secured the services of a layperson to work with the pastor in building up the quality of adult fellowship in the church. As he and the pastor discussed the scope of his work and the things he might do, the list grew unwieldy. He was to bring groups together, come up with program ideas, lead mission trips, visit new members, and recruit volunteers. "I'm not sure what we should call you," the pastor said. "We could put 'Lay Minister' on your business card or something like that."

As the discussion went on, the focus shifted to the need for building up the people of the congregation and the quality of fellowship in the church. Jokingly, the man said, "Why don't we just put 'People Builder'?" And it was done. As far as I know, this lay minister is the only professional church lay worker with a business card that says anything like it: "Gregory Mason: People Builder." What a wonderful illustration of the biblical injunction to "encourage one another and build up each other, as indeed you are doing" (1 Thessalonians 5:11).

Introducing new technological tools for ministry in the life of a church is an opportunity to bring new people into ministry. God has given gifts to every member of the Body of Christ to help build up the church. While these gifts have been translated into gifts of teaching, leading the children of the church, preaching, administration, and a multitude of others, there are all kinds of people with gifts that have yet to be used.

A woman in a central Wisconsin congregation was reading her church newsletter and the pastor's request for someone with Power-

Point knowledge to assist with a new project. This woman and her family were not very regular in their church attendance and were not involved in any form of ministry. She volunteered for the project on a limited basis. She helped to develop PowerPoint illustrations and find movie clips that would illustrate sermon themes for a new worship service the pastor was introducing. Two and a half years later, she works each week with a team putting together film clips and PowerPoint presentations. Her entire family, including teenage children, spends time each week thinking about Christian themes in contemporary film and television. Her teens have begun to work with other teens in the church to put together their own presentations.

People who discover meaningful involvement in the life of the church and its ministry will grow in their commitment to Christ and the church. This not only makes for stronger disciples, but will bring about more effective evangelism when these folks talk to others about the things they are doing. The teens who began working on PowerPoint presentations in that Wisconsin church very naturally drew their friends into their work.

People are the force that will make this new ministry work. Program is the vehicle by which you will bring the ministry to the church. The program component of your new ministry will include developing a plan, a budget, and a time frame. In chapter 11 I discussed the importance of a planning team for developing ways to introduce new technologies for worship. By "planning," I mean that which takes place when a church is beginning to consider bringing new technologies into the ministry of the church. This is a critical step for congregations that are just beginning to move into the area of technology and ministry. If your group has already ventured into this ministry and does not yet have an overall plan involving persons besides the pastoral staff, you should create one as soon as possible.

Program

As you develop a plan for your congregation, there are some important questions to ask. The following list of questions will help you get started. I have discussed many of these things in earlier chapters. The object is to bring together the things you've learned and develop an overall plan for your ministry context. The next chapter has several ideas for use in the local church, but these will help to jump-start your discussions. Every local situation is unique, and your planning group will craft its own solution for the church's ministry.

"What Technologies Are Available?"
- Email for communications
- Internet access for study and research
- LCD projectors to project; videocassette, DVD, and computer files
- Web site

"Where Could We Use These Technologies?"
- Sunday school classes
- Youth group
- Adult studies
- Worship
- Committee meetings
- Church office
- Pastor's office

"How Could We Use These Technologies?"
- A Sunday school class can make use of software for Christian education that is available for the personal computer. If Internet access is available for the Sunday school, classes can communicate with missionaries or study material found on the Internet. Children who have Internet access in their homes can continue with their Christian education studies throughout the week by using material provided on the church's Web site.
- A youth group could use Internet access, design a Web site, develop PowerPoint presentations, and more. (In other words, it could likely use anything the church is able to provide!)
- Adult studies could be augmented through email communication. With Internet access at church and in members' homes, adult learning could take place entirely online.

- Using PowerPoint presentations in portions of the service can enhance worship. A worship service could also be completely organized around a multimedia presentation.
- Committee meetings could use PowerPoint and an LCD projector for agendas and reports.
- The church office could make use of email for communication among members, Internet access to denominational materials, art for newsletters, and Web authoring software for a church Web site.
- The pastor could make use of email for communication with members, colleagues, and denominational personnel. Internet access would provide the pastor with research and study help for the preaching and teaching ministry.

Pieces

The final component in your plan is to obtain the "pieces" for the program. With an overview in hand of what you hope to accomplish, you can begin thinking about the equipment you will need to move ahead with technology in ministry.

"WHAT EQUIPMENT WILL WE NEED?"

Before you actually compile the list of equipment you need, it is necessary to make a list of ministry priorities. If you could accomplish just one thing after working through the ideas in this chapter, what would it be? Create your list of priorities and take good notes during your discussions. When the time comes for budgeting, the work of writing a proposal with goals, objectives, and a rationale for investment in your tech program will be greatly simplified.

Possibly the goal of your group will be to have the ability to move into all the areas we have covered. In order to have this capability, you will need the following hardware items:

- A laptop computer
- An LCD projector
- A VCR or DVD player

This equipment is really not too expensive, and you could likely borrow the VCR. The scope of your eventual program needs will determine just what kind of equipment inventory you will need. A single computer with Internet access in a Sunday school would provide the means for email communication with missionaries. If teaching software is used for the class, one computer for every three children works well. One LCD projector will serve the needs of a medium-size congregation. If both worship and Sunday school will make extensive use of the LCD projector, you may want to plan to purchase a second one in a future budget. As with other technological equipment, the price of LCD projectors has dropped steadily over the past two years and should continue to be affordable in the foreseeable future.

In addition to the hardware, you will need a presentation software such as PowerPoint and Web authoring software such as FrontPage.

DEVELOPING A BUDGET

Several factors will determine how you go about planning a budget for purchasing the equipment and software you will need for your church. A review of chapter 6 will help.

Excursus: About the Small Church— Technology for Everybody

Before I move into budget planning for new technology, I need to mention a specific issue for smaller congregations. Many small churches struggle to simply make ends meet. More and more of these congregations are served by seminary students and lay pastors.

"How does any of this tech stuff apply to us?" one student asked. She was computer literate and very interested in applying educational technologies in the congregation she served, but the money just wasn't available to purchase equipment. She managed to come up with a solution that made technologies for ministry realistic for any congregation. Here's how. The PowerPoint program was available at the seminary and through The United Methodist Church. She prepared a very effective presentation entitled "God's Creation." She was able to borrow an LCD projector from her local library. The congregation loved the result, and a few of the members talked about how this could be effective in their ministry with the few young people they have in the church. A small group of congregations are now discussing the possibility of forming a consortium to purchase equipment that will be shared.

Technology is increasingly available to most congregations at reasonable expense. There are no longer substantive barriers to any congregation that wishes to get on board with the new technologies.

It is time to develop a technology budget for your ministry. Here's your first step:

- Complete an inventory of the computer and media equipment you already have.
- Note the cost of maintaining and replacing the equipment in the inventory.

The second step in the process is to examine your current equipment inventory. What equipment has to be repaired or replaced? Set the cost of this aside while you consider purchasing new equipment. Use the discussion of equipment in chapter 6 to help with your analysis.

The third phase of developing a budget plan is to spell out the cost of a basic equipment inventory that can meet your needs. The following list is an example of a minimum inventory that could accomplish most of the objectives noted above.

1. Laptop computer $1,800 (This should purchase a laptop that comes with a DVD player.)
2. LCD projector $3,000 (A minimum 1,100-lumen projector recommended.)
3. Screen $ 400 (If you do not already have one, I suggest a floor-mount model.)
4. VCR $ 99 (or borrow one)
5. Software $ 400 (You can likely find this cheaper.)

This is a list of minimum equipment and software you will need. New computers usually come with some software, but you should have a line item for programs such as PowerPoint. When you consider what these tools can accomplish, $5,699 is an exceptional value. If you already own a screen, can secure the software through your denomination or school for around $199, and borrow the VCR, you save $700 and are on your way for just under $5,000.[1]

When you purchase the minimum inventory needed to begin your program, it is akin to buying the basic model when you purchase an automobile. Staying with the analogy, it is possible to get the nicely equipped model of your technological inventory for $8,000–$9,000. This would buy a laptop computer with a few more bells and whistles, a more powerful LCD projector, a rollabout cart for the system, and a good set of speakers for the projector.

There is one last budget item that those who develop the financial proposal for purchasing new tools in ministry should recognize. An adequate office for today's pastors should include a computer with Internet access. Research and study materials, denominational resources, and electronic communication are some of the great bargains of the past few decades. A good library and continuing education expenses are without a doubt the most significant contributions that can be made toward effective pastoral ministry. Many pastors simply cannot afford the books and continuing education classes it takes to remain effective in ministry. If a congregation were to do nothing else, it would improve its life by providing a decent computer with Internet access for the pastor. The computer will cost $1,500 or less, and the Internet access will be approximately $250 for the year. If cable access is available and you can afford it, the cost is very much worthwhile. The computer should be no more than two years old. Undoubtedly someone will comment, "But we just bought a new computer four years ago!" Tell the person a four-year-old computer is the equivalent of a forty-year-old car. A small investment in giving the pastor access to expanded resources for preaching and teaching will have a positive and lasting impact on the life of the church.

Chapter Thirteen

Ideas You Can Use in Your Local Church

Pastor's Email Newsletter

I will take a bit more time to discuss the email newsletter because email is one of the easiest tools to use.

Earlier I mentioned Pastor Ken Bickel of the First Congregational United Church of Christ in Dubuque, Iowa. He diligently gathers email addresses from parishioners and once or twice a week sends a brief note announcing church events, special occasions, prayer requests, and birthday and anniversary greetings. When a member who has an email address is mentioned, Pastor Bickel encourages others to write to him or her and includes the person's email address in his note. In order to use this and other email group ideas, you will need to learn how to set up a group in your email program. When you send a note to the group, it goes to everyone on the list. With a very large list, it is best to send the email to your own email address and put everyone else in the group in the BCC (blind copy) heading. This way the whole list of email addresses will not show up on each person's email message.

Parishioners are grateful for their pastor's work on this means of pastoral care. He received the following note: "Dear Ken, thank you for all the emails. They really help to stay connected to the church. I often am away on weekends and the emails help me keep up-to-date and stay in touch with others. I have posted copies of your email to several of my friends in Davenport. They are trying to convince their pastors to get online."

Here is a copy of one of his notes (the email addresses and names have been changed):

> **Dear Church Members,**
>
> **"As the Father has loved me, so I have loved you; abide in my love" (John 15:9).**
>
> **As a church family we always seek to abide in the love of God. I encourage you to support one another and to uphold one another in the faith by worshiping together and by praying for one another, always showing love and kindness to your brothers and sisters in the faith.**
>
> **Many in our church family need our support this evening. Jane Smith had her tonsils removed this afternoon at Mercy Hospital. Dr. Ralph Brown messed up his ankle in a waterskiing accident while on vacation last Wednesday. Ralph was able to make it to church with his crutches, but he will certainly be challenged in taking two daughters off to college and in doing surgery this week. Please keep all of these individuals in your prayers!**
>
> **Our Chicago youth and adult crew made it home safely Sunday evening. They had a wonderful worship experience during their trip to Chicago and will have lots to tell us about next Sunday.**
>
> **Rose McDonald turned seventy today! You can e-mail her at *jayie@now.com*. Joe and Sandy Hansen will celebrate their 30th wedding anniversary. You can e-mail them at *rrln@city.com*.**
>
>

Have a great day!
Ken Bickel
>

Pastor Bickel finds his work on the email newsletter a worthwhile investment of time and an extension of his pastoral care. Some church members have gotten online partly because of this work.

Consistency and persistence are critical for the success of this tool. He has patiently developed this form of ministry over the past three years. Pastor Bickel's success with this newsletter also depends on his regularly checking and answering his email.

Email Lectionary or Sermon Preparation/Study Group Material

Recruit a group of persons in your congregation who have email access and who agree to help study and reflect on the lectionary passages. For those who do not use the lectionary, the following Sunday's scripture texts can be used. Each Monday, the pastor will send out the passages for the following Sunday with a few reflections and questions. The members of the group read the texts and share their thoughts and questions using email and the Reply to All function. This way all members of the group will receive all the messages.

Ask that group members complete discussion by Wednesday. This creates a keen sense of interest in the Sunday sermons for those who participate. If there are enough people with email access, it helps to recruit new members for the weekly discussions. Share some of the discussion with the congregation to engender additional interest in using email.

Email Sunshine Committee

Many churches have a person who sends out birthday and anniversary cards. (Don't do away with handwritten, personal notes.) Some churches have a committee of persons who take on this ministry. The work of this group could be expanded by a weekly message sent to persons with email access. This message could be a short devotional or inspirational thought to point persons toward God's ever-present love.

Committee and Administrative Uses

When using email and the Internet gains visibility in the church, the number of members using these tools will grow. Some of the ways congregations effectively use email include disbursing meeting minutes and discussing committee items. As Internet use grows, email can help reduce paper communication. (And save a few trees in the process.) Even if only a small percentage of people who make up a committee or board use email, the church office can put them in email groups and save on the time it takes to make individual phone calls. In a highly mobile society, there are times when groups have difficulty setting meeting times. With the expanding use of email, and the ability to access email accounts from almost any location, it is possible for people to participate in decision making through email even when they cannot be present at a meeting.

Yahoo! Groups

Yahoo! Groups is a very powerful free tool offered by Yahoo! Inc., one of the first search engines on the Internet. Yahoo! Groups can be used by Sunday school classes, youth groups, adult study groups, and almost any organization within the church. Some of the features include group email, the ability to customize a group homepage without knowing HTML, and chat. The nice thing about the chat room is that when you create a group for members only, the chat function is quite secure and outside folks cannot spy on or participate in the conversations. A Yahoo! group would be a good way to introduce chat in a secure environment to a group of younger folks in the church. These groups can serve as anything from a Bible study group to a recipe exchange or church cookbook committee. Discussions are saved in archives that can be visited anytime.

Visit the Internet site *http://groups.yahoo.com* to become familiar with the opportunities that are offered without charge.

Blackboard.com

The Web site blackboard.com is an excellent Internet resource. Here you can create and teach a class. Pastors, Sunday school teachers, and youth group leaders can use blackboard.com in creative ways that can offer a genuine extension of the local church's educational ministry.[1]

Student and instructor manuals are available online. A visit to *www.blackboard.com* is necessary to become acquainted with this resource's powerful features. More than sixty-five hundred universities and schools now use the Blackboard learning platform. Denominations and judicatories will likely look into the licensed version of Blackboard's learning platform for creating and offering educational opportunities.

Use Yahoo! Groups and Blackboard in the Wider Church

Local churches of the same denomination could link their confirmation classes together by using Yahoo! Groups or Blackboard. This could be especially helpful when a local church does not have enough students to form a viable class. Assignments can be made and discussions required. A Blackboard course site could become a complete online course. Blackboard also includes a chat function and the ability to post Web links for research and study.

Clergy groups could use Yahoo! Groups or Blackboard to build collegiality, offer mutual support, conduct consultations, or hold discussions on topics of mutual interest. There are hundreds of groups already in existence on these sites centered around Christian faith, youth work, clergy concerns, and Bible study.

Ways to Use Video

A small camera for your laptop computer costs less than $100 and can be used in a variety of ways. Here are just a few:

- Because the laptop computer is portable, it could be taken to a nursing home or the home of a shut-in. A brief message could be recorded and shown through the LCD projector just before prayer time in worship, at a meeting of the women's circle, or in a Sunday school class.

- Archive video files of Sunday school children singing some of their favorite songs. Do new files each year during the children's elementary school years and use these videos in a confirmation service when each group of children is confirmed. A number of brief video files can be stored on a CD and given to each family.

- PC-compatible cameras come with software that can be used to create photos that can be sent by means of email to others. Use the Internet to find other Sunday schools and youth groups on the Internet and use this new method to form a community of "pen pals."

- One of the fastest ways to bring email use to grandparents in the church is to hold a workshop in which they learn to use email in order to receive photos of grandchildren.

- CDs can contain a combination of video and document files to use in capital campaigns or the annual budget. These could be especially effective for members who live out of town or who for other reasons cannot be present at meetings where the ministry and mission of the church are presented. CD production is less expensive than videotape and compares favorably with audiocassettes. Given the superior video capability of CDs, the choice will eventually become the CD.

- For churches and organizations that are considering more extensive use of video, there is exciting news about the available technologies. Biblical themes and stories can be brought to life with a youth group video-production project. Chances are that one or more of the young people in a church have access to a computer that is capable of video production. A regular videocassette recorder can be converted into digital signal and processed in a computer. Digital camcorders provide excellent-quality video and are becoming much less expensive. One of the striking changes in technological tools is in the field of video editing and even film production. Ten years ago, film production required hundreds of thousands of dollars just to purchase equipment. Five years ago a film could be produced for fifty thousand dollars. Technology to produce a good-quality video can be purchased today for $7,500. A youth group could produce a nice-quality amateur video with equipment and software that cost just under $1,000. The key to video production is a computer with lots of RAM and a fast processor.[2]

Ways to Use the Internet[3]

Internet access will open up an amazing resource for study, research, professional development, and support for virtually every area of church life. Some of the biggest benefits will be:

- Study resources for pastors. The Web site *www.ccel.org* stands out because of its wealth of scholarly resources. Here you can find the complete library of Early Church Fathers from the Ante-Nicene Fathers to the Nicene and Post-Nicene Fathers. Also available is the World Wide Encyclopedia of Christianity where you can study the Nestorian controversy or visit the World Wide Study Bible and find material from several Bible dictionaries covering every book of the Bible.
- Sunday school teachers will find a wealth of materials from denominational resources. A particularly valuable site, according to many students and teachers, is the Web site of the Workshop Rotation Model of Sunday school. The site, located at *www.rotation.org,* is a growing resource of lesson plans and ideas for churches using a workshop model for Sunday school. This site, with its links, will become a major resource for many Sunday schools.
- Information about most denominations is available on the Internet. This information can become a valuable resource for Sunday school and confirmation classes. Teachers can make assignments to pairs or groups of students to encourage collab-

orative learning. Email can be used to facilitate the completion of homework assignments.

- Search engines will provide access to resources for Bible study, Christian parenting discussion groups, worship resources, or information on world missions. My current recommendation is to begin with the search engine at *www.google.com.*

Ways to Use an Internet Presence

The Internet presents an opportunity for a church to publish its mission, program, and schedule for much less than print media would cost. The ways to do this are limited only by the imagination of those who commit themselves to ministry in this area. A small sampling of ways to use an Internet presence are:

- Create a basic brochure about the church and its activities. Include photographs of current staff and activities. The brochure is a twenty-four-hour presence that includes all the information a visitor would need in order to visit the congregation.
- Consider a "launch day" fellowship event for the congregation at which the members are the first persons to see the church's Web site. Connect your portable computer to the Internet and project the Web site through the LCD projector. A "launch day" event can bring the church together around the idea of your Web presence as ministry.
- Provide a "virtual" tour of the church by providing photographs and an email link to the pastor or other representatives of the church with an offer for one of these persons to meet the visitor on Sunday morning. Remember that a visit to your church by means of the Internet is the least threatening way possible to visit a church.
- Challenge the church's youth group to create a youth section to the church's Web presence that will reach out to other young people. Have the group post personal comments and insights on community, school, and social issues.

- Create a church membership directory with email links so that members can communicate easily with others. Protect this area with a password to a "members only" section of the site.
- As the Web site is developed, allow opportunity online for members and others to sign up for classes and other events through the Web site. Most Web authoring programs will help with the forms function.
- Create a page for prayer requests and mutual support for members.
- Create a page of links to denominational, Christian parenting, Bible study, and other informational Web sites.
- Develop one section of the Web site as a community resource where persons in your larger community will visit often. This can become the beginning of your outreach or evangelism program.
- When you have secured a domain name for your church, be sure to publish your Web address (URL) on every letterhead, bulletin, newspaper ad, Yellow Pages ad, and any other places your church name appears in print.

These ideas represent a few of the possibilities that await you as you develop your ministry using some of the technological tools available today. Hopefully, you have discovered that although the field of technology is a major force in contemporary culture and necessarily in the church, it is not all that mysterious after all. None of us can do everything that is possible with these new tools. In fact, we cannot even begin to know all there is to know or develop all the skills there are to develop. But each of us can take a piece of this huge puzzle and work together to bring some exciting new dimensions to the ministry of our churches.

All books have a final page and when you have read that page, you can shelve the book. I hope for two things. First, that you will not shelve this book at all, but will pass it on. Second, remember that this book will be updated through the companion Web site at *www.newtools-online.com*. When you arrive at the site, you will find the links I recommend organized according to the chapters in this book. The prices of computers and other equipment will likely change before you read this book, but through the companion Web site you will be able to stay current.

An even more exciting prospect is the opportunity to share with others some of the creative ways you will use the materials in this book. Like many students I have known, many of you will go on to develop and implement some marvelous new ways of serving the church and reaching out. You will, without a doubt, accomplish greater things than you thought possible when you first wondered what in the world a URL was.

I hope that many of you will consider submitting some of the ways you are implementing technology in your church's ministry. Visit the companion Web site for instructions on how to do this. It will be possible to share many of those ideas with your brothers and sisters who are working along with you to discover more effective ways of teaching, preaching, and building up the family of God. When you get to the New Tools Web site, you will find directions for joining with others in a discussion group for people who are beginning to implement new technologies in their local church ministries.

Appendix

Skip Quiz #1

Computer Basics

CPU stands for:

☐ Computer Program Union
☐ Computer Parts Uniformity
☐ Central Processing Unit
☐ Conditional Process Uniface

RAM stands for:

☐ Real-time Active Mode
☐ Random Access Memory
☐ Read and Manipulate
☐ Readiness Activity Mode

The speed of a computer is determined by:

☐ The size of the hard drive
☐ The model of printer being used
☐ The MHz of the processing chip
☐ The electrical service in your home

Which of the following is *not* necessary to make your computer run?

☐ An operating system
☐ A central processing unit
☐ A hard drive
☐ A CD-RW drive

Which of the following holds more information?
☐ A floppy disc
☐ A ZIP disc
☐ A CD
☐ A serial port

You can speed up your computer by adding more RAM.
☐ TRUE   ☐ FALSE

Most computers have at least two operating systems.
☐ TRUE   ☐ FALSE

PCs can use only Microsoft software.
☐ TRUE   ☐ FALSE

The terms *PC* and *Macintosh* are interchangeable.
☐ TRUE   ☐ FALSE

The personal computer was invented by Bill Gates.
☐ TRUE   ☐ FALSE

Most computers today run on DOS.
☐ TRUE   ☐ FALSE

Which of the following are essential components of a basic computer system?
☐ A monitor
☐ A hard drive
☐ A keyboard
☐ A scanner

Which of the following are types of printers?
☐ Dot matrix
☐ Ink-jet
☐ Thermograph
☐ Laser

Answer Key for Skip Quiz #1

CPU stands for:
Central Processing Unit (measured in MHz; called the "chip")

RAM stands for:
Random Access Memory

The speed of a computer is determined by:
The MHz (megahertz) of the processing chip (Pentium II, Pentium III, Pentium 4, Celeron, AMD)

Which of the following is *not* necessary to make your computer run?
A CD-RW drive. The CD drive is either ROM or RW. The ROM is a "read-only" drive, and most programs come on CD. The CD-RW is a drive that can write on CDs as well as read them. You do not need a drive that will write discs in order to make your computer run.

Which of the following holds more information?
A CD. The CD holds 650 MB of information, the ZIP drive either 100 or 250 MB, and the floppy disc holds 1.45 MB. The serial port is one way to connect a device with the computer. It has nothing to do with memory.

You can speed up your computer by adding more RAM.
True.

Most computers have at least two operating systems.
False. (The operating system will likely be Microsoft Windows. There are others, but *never* two.)

PCs can use only Microsoft software.
False. (Although Microsoft has a very large segment of the software market, there are literally hundreds of software companies that manufacture software for the PC.)

The terms *PC* and *Macintosh* are interchangeable.
False. (*Big* false! It's one or the other.)

The personal computer was invented by Bill Gates.
False. (Bill Gates's Microsoft is a *software* company. The PC is *hardware*.)

Most computers today run on DOS.
False. (DOS stands for "Disc Operating System." It is an older operating system for the PC that was replaced by Microsoft Windows.)

Which of the following are essential components of a basic computer system?
A monitor, a hard drive, and a keyboard. (The scanner is an optional piece of equipment that is used to scan text or graphics into a computer file, which can then be used in your documents or Web pages.)

Which of the following are types of printers?
Dot matrix, ink-jet, and laser.

Skip Quiz #2

Internet Basics

URL stands for:
- [ ] Unlimited Range Library
- [ ] Understood Regulatory Limit
- [ ] Uniform Resource Locator
- [ ] Undeveloped Response Language

A computer that shows your Web site to the rest of the world is a:
- [ ] Client
- [ ] Macintosh
- [ ] Server
- [ ] PC

HTML is:
- [ ] A type of computer used to design a Web site
- [ ] A Web browser
- [ ] A software program designed by Microsoft
- [ ] A language that tells a browser how to display Internet pages

FTP is:
- [ ] A program for designing Web pages
- [ ] A special computer chip
- [ ] A program for sending files to another computer
- [ ] A Web site

Which of the following is *not* necessary to build and deploy a Web page?
- ☐ A computer
- ☐ A domain name
- ☐ A server
- ☐ Access to the Internet

A browser is a program that displays code in text and images.
   ☐ TRUE   ☐ FALSE

Microsoft Internet Explorer is a browser.
   ☐ TRUE   ☐ FALSE

Microsoft FrontPage is a browser.
   ☐ TRUE   ☐ FALSE

The Internet is located in Washington, D.C.
   ☐ TRUE   ☐ FALSE

If false:
Where *is* the Internet located? _____

The Internet was begun by Bill Gates.
   ☐ TRUE   ☐ FALSE

There is no way to tell what sites have been visited by a computer.
   ☐ TRUE   ☐ FALSE

Which of the following are ways to communicate with people using the computer? (Choose one or more.)
- ☐ Email
- ☐ Search engines
- ☐ Chat
- ☐ Windows

Answer Key for Skip Quiz #2

URL stands for:
Uniform Resource Locator (the Internet equivalent of an address)

A computer that shows your Web site to the rest of the world is a:
Server. (Think of it as being similar to your server at the restaurant. This server feeds information to computers that come looking for information.)

HTML is:
A language that tells a browser how to display Internet pages. (HTML stands for "hypertext markup language." Codes are written right along with the information to tell the computer's browser how to display the information.)

FTP is:
A program for sending files to another computer. (FTP stands for "File Transfer Protocol." You want to *transfer* files from your computer to another computer—say a server—and you need to follow a *protocol* to get them there safely.)

Which of the following is *not* necessary to build and deploy a Web page?
A domain name. (A domain name would be *www.myname.com*; the *myname* part is a domain name. You don't need one to build a Web page and place it on a server.)

A browser is a program that displays code in text and images.
True.

Microsoft Internet Explorer is a browser.
True.

Microsoft FrontPage is a browser.
False. (FrontPage is a program that helps you write Web pages.)

The Internet is located in Washington, D.C.
False.

Where *is* the Internet located?
There is no physical location. (The Internet is global—wherever computers are communicating with one another. Thus the name "Web," like a spider web.)

The Internet was begun by Bill Gates.
False.

There is no way to tell what sites have been visited by a computer.
False. (Every parent will want to know how to look at the history part of the browser's menu bar, *and* how to look at the cookies or footprints visited sites leave in your computer's temporary files.)

Which of the following are ways to communicate with people using the computer? (Choose one or more.)
Email, chat

Web Site Planning Sheets

Planning Your Web Presence

A. Why?

Brainstorm Ideas

Visit Other Church Sites

Visit Areas of Ministry

Write a Clear Mission Statement

Planning Your Web Presence

A. Why?

Brainstorm Ideas

- To publicize our church
- To educate
- To reach new people
- To inform members
- To serve the community

Visit Other Church Sites

- *www.upc.org*   *Things we like; things we want to avoid*
- *www.lakeave.org*
- *http://churches.net/churches/*
  (Here you can look up a number of churches.)

Visit Areas of Ministry

- Pastoral ministry (pastor will do a column/sermons).
- Youth (youth group will edit a youth section).
- Education (Sunday school may add lesson sheets for parents at a later time).
- Outreach (may consider posting family resources for other needed resources).
- Social Concerns (this is not ready at this time, but church may want to post pledge forms).

Write a Clear Mission Statement

Think through clearly what you want the mission of Internet ministry to be. It may be limited or extensive, but make it clear.

- The Web site of First Church will serve as our Internet brochure with a message from the pastor, current worship times, and program notes.
- The Web site of First Church will serve the community as a major source of information for senior citizens, reach out to unchurched people with an interactive forum on family issues, provide our members with member-only information, and provide persons who are seeking a church home with extensive information and interactive opportunities to get to know our congregation.

Planning Your Web Presence

B. Who?

Who will author the site?

Who will provide material?

Who will update the site?

Who will make policy for the site?

Planning Your Web Presence

B. Who?

Who will author the site?

- Will one person do the authoring, or will the site be authored by a team?
- Do we have a person or persons who know how to do this?
- What kind of training is available?
- Where can we find online resources for authoring?

Who will provide material?

- Who will provide material for the site? (Be sure to figure time requirements if you plan to use current staff.)
- What format will we follow in gathering material?
- Realistically—how much material can we regularly use in light of time requirements?

Who will update the site?

- Who will update the site? (Do not post a site until this question is fully answered!)
- How often will the updates be made? (This will help determine the content that should be included.)
- A monthly calendar means monthly updates, a weekly calendar means weekly updates, and so on.

Who will make policy for the site?

- Establish clear lines of responsibility for what should go on the site and who will make editorial decisions.
- Should this be:
  —the pastor
  —the editor?
  —the Web ministry team?
  —the author or authors?

Planning Your Web Presence

C. How?

How will we author the site?

How do we name our site?

How do we publish our site?

How do we *grow* our site?

Planning Your Web Presence

C. How?

How will we author the site?

- Easiest—get free Web space at a site such as *www.forministry.com.*
- Easy—use Microsoft Word and save as HTML, FrontPage Express (free at the Microsoft Web site).
- Harder—FrontPage and other Web authoring tools; free: Arachnophilia and 1st Page
- Hardest—HTML coding, Java, Flash

How do we name our site?

- If we use free space, the name of the site is given.
- In ISP-hosted sites, we name the extension.
- If we buy a domain name (*www.ourchurch.org*), we pay $35 per year to own the name. (This is called a "virtual domain." The advantage is that we keep the same name, and it's an easy-to-remember name no matter where our site is located.)

How do we publish our site?

- With free space, the site is published when we complete the information, as with forministry.com.
- With Web page compilers like FrontPage, the program has a publishing wizard to lead through the publishing steps.

How do we *grow* our site?

- To expand site use online resources.
- *www.htmlgoodies.com*
- *www.mvd.com/webguide*
- Information/Web dictionary—*www.webopedia.com*
- Graphics—*www.clipart.com*
- Good search engine: *www.google.com*

Notes

Introduction: "Toto, I've a Feeling We're Not in Kansas Anymore"

1. Daniel S. Goldin, "UVA Newsmakers," May 29, 2001 <*http://www.virginia.edu/uvanewsmakers/newsmakers/goldin.html*> (September 17, 2001).

Chapter One: Really, Really Basic Computer Stuff

1. Hereafter commonly referred to as Microsoft Windows.

Chapter Two: Really, Really Basic Internet Stuff

1. Robert H. Zakon, *Hobbes' Internet Timeline*, August 23, 2001 <*http://www.zakon.org/robert/internet/timeline*> (September 17, 2001).
2. Microsoft Internet Explorer® is either a registered trademark or a trademark of Microsoft Corporation in the United States and/or other countries.

Chapter Three: Would Jesus Carry a Pager?

1. Angela R. Garber, "Make a Statement," *Small Business Computing,* February 2001, p. 29.
2. Barna Research Online, "The Cyberchurch Is Coming," April 20, 1998 <*www.barna.org*> (August 21, 2001).

3. Dennis McCafferty, "Between Heaven and Cyberspace," *USA Weekend,* March 17–19, 2000, p. 14.

4. Ibid.

5. I will talk about exactly how to do this in chapter 13.

6. From the Westfield Center *<http://www.westfield.org/curious.htm>* (August 24, 2001). The Westfield Center, founded in 1979, is an association for organ performers/scholars.

7. Pew Internet and American Life, "Teenage Life Online," June 20, 2001 *<http://www.pewinternet.org/reports/reports.asp?Report=36&Section =ReportLevel2&Field=Level2ID&ID=188>* (September 17, 2001).

Chapter Four: How the Landscape Has Changed

1. Robert H. Zakon, *Hobbes' Internet Timeline* v5.3, July 17, 2001 *<http://www.zakon.org/robert/internet/timeline>* (July 17, 2001).

2. Ibid.

3. Television Bureau of Advertising, Inc. *<http://www.tvb.org/tvfacts/tvbasics /basics1.html>* (July 18, 2001).

4. National Center for Education Statistics: Statistics in Brief, "Internet Access in U.S. Public Schools and Classrooms: 1994-2000," May 2001 *<http://nces.ed.gov /pubs2001/2001071.pdf>* (September 11, 2001).

5. Marianne McGee, "It's Official: IT Adds Up," *Information Week,* April 17, 2000, no. 782, p. 42, or *<http://www.informationweek.com/782/productivity.htm>* (August 17, 2001).

6. United States Department of Education "Emerging Priorities," May 1, 2000 *<http://www.air.org/forum/issues.htm>* (July 30, 2001).

7. "The ICN Story," September 17, 2001 *<http://www.icn.state.ia.us/HTMLDOCS /story/history.html>* (September 17, 2001).

Chapter Five: For Parents and Pastors

1. Pew Internet and American Life, "A General Portrait of Wired Teens," June 20, 2001 *<http://www.pewinternet.org/reports/reports.asp?Report=36&Section =ReportLevel2ID&ID=200>* (September 17, 2001).

2. See ERIC Digests, "Guidelines for Family Television Viewing," September 17, 2001 *<http://www.ed.gov/databases/ERIC_Digests/ed320662.html>* (September 17, 2001).

3. Blue Ridge Thunder, "ThunderShots," March 2001 *<http://www.blueridgethunder .com>* (September 17, 2001).

4. Ibid.

5. "Kyl Calling It Quits?" *Player's Advocate,* November 4, 2000 <*http://www*
.*playersadvocate.com/kyle.html*> (July 18, 2001).

6. Keith J. Anderson, Ph.D., "Internet Use Among College Students: An Exploratory Study," July 18, 2001 <*http://www.rpi.edu/~anderk4/research.html*> (July 18, 2001).

7. Visit the companion Web site *www.newtools-online.com* for an example of a short quiz on Internet addiction.

8. University of Michigan Health System, "Alcohol Use: Teenage Drinking," September 17, 2001 <*http://www.med.umich.edu/1libr/subabuse/alcuse03.htm*> (September 17, 2001).

9. The Web site *www.safekids.com* is must reading as soon as you have Internet access.

10. You will find some of the better ones listed on the companion Web site *www.newtools-online.com.*

11. See also the companion site *www.newtools-online.com* for more links pertaining to family computing.

12. Mike Anton and Lisa Ryckman, "In Hindsight, Signs to Killings Obvious," May 2, 1999 <*http://denver.rockymountainnews.com/shooting/0502why10.shtml*> (September 17, 2001).

13. From the Game Deputy Web site <*http://www.deputysoftware.com/circle/eadamsprint.html*>.

14. Pew Internet and American Life, "Who's Not Online: 57% of Those Without Internet Access Say They Do Not Plan to Log On," September 21, 2000 <*http://www.pewinternet.org/reports/pdfs/Pew_Those_Not_Online_Report.pdf*> (July 18, 2001).

15. Ibid.

16. *Pew Internet and American Life,* "Wired Churches, Wired Temples: Taking Congregations and Missions Into Cyberspace," December 20, 2000 <*http://www.pewinternet.org*> (July 18, 2001).

17. Go to the companion Web site *www.newtools-online.com* for a "quick start" list of links for Sunday school leaders.

Chapter Six: Audiovisuals with a New Twist

1. The complete article is available at <*http://www.sunlink.ucf.edu/pub/spr98/200.html*>.

2. A handy inflation calculator is available at <*http://www.westegg.com/inflation*>.

3. Personally, when it comes to family news or a birthday card, I still prefer Mom's handwriting and having something I can hold in my hands over the short, even terse, email greetings my techie friends send.

4. See *www.rotation.org* for examples.

5. The companion Web site *www.newtools-online.com* contains links that will help in your research.

Chapter Seven: More About Software: PowerPoint

1. Microsoft FrontPage® is either a registered trademark or trademark of Microsoft Corporation in the United States and/or other countries.
2. There is a section of PowerPoint resources on the companion Web site *www.newtools-online.com.*

Chapter Eight: More About Software: Creating a Web Presence

1. The companion Web site *www.newtools-online.com* has some links to simple tutorials on writing HTML.
2. The URL is *<http://www.uct.ac.za/depts/its/webdesign/build/install.htm #DownloadingFP>*.
3. The companion Web site *www.newtools-online.com* has information on securing a free copy of an FTP program for churches.

Chapter Nine: Internet-Based Ministry: Planning

1. When you are searching for a host for your virtual domain, I recommend that you check with *www.genevaonline.com*. The prices and reliability of its service are very good. There is a link to its service and more information on the companion Web site *www.newtools-online.com.*

Chapter Ten: Christian Education and Youth Ministry

1. U.S. Department of Education, "From Digital Divide to Digital Opportunity: A National Call to Action," June 20, 2000 *<http://www.ed.gov/Technology /dunn-form.html>* August 10, 2001.
2. Kennedy Space Center, "Shuttle Mission Archive," September 27, 2000 *<www-pao.ksc.nasa.gov/kscpao/shuttle/missions/sts-2/mission-sts-2.html>* (September 18, 2001).
3. This project could be carried out with the equipment specified, along with a screen and an LCD projector. Even without the new technology, it could be done with a video screen, 35mm slides, and an audiocassette recorder.

4. There is an example on the companion Web site *www.newtools-online.com* of a movie called *The Resurrection Project,* which was written and produced by a youth group.

Chapter Eleven: Media Arts in Worship

1. Available at *<http://www.csse.monash.edu.au/~pringle/silent/>*.
2. A history of the early film industry is available at the Encyclopaedia Britannica Web site. See *<http://www.britannica.com/eb/article?eu =119924&tocid=52135>* and *<http://www.britannica.com/eb/article?eu=119925 &tocid=52139>*.
3. A copy of these exercises is available to print out on the companion Web site *www.newtools-online.com.*

Chapter Twelve: Three Central Components: People, Program, and Pieces

1. The cost of these products can change so rapidly that you will want to check the figures on the companion Web site *www.newtools-online.com* before preparing a final budget.

Chapter Thirteen: Ideas You Can Use in Your Local Church

1. Yahoo! Groups and blackboard.com are offering their services at this time. Any changes will be updated on the companion Web site *www.newtools-online .com.*
2. Check the companion Web site for links to the latest information on video equipment and information on video production. Documentation of a project called *The Resurrection Project,* done by a small local church youth group, is also posted on the site.
3. All of the Web sites listed are also linked on the companion Web site along with additional resources.